Sarria to

A Guide to walking the last 100km of the Camino Francés

M. J. McCarthy

Copyright
All rights reserved. With the exception of the maps which are Copyright OpenStreetMap Contributors and are therefore Open Licence, no part of this book may be reproduced in any form or by any electronic or mechanical means including information storage and retrieval systems except in the case of brief quotations in articles or reviews without the permission in writing from its publisher, Mark McCarthy.

All brand names and product names used in this book are trademarks, registered trademarks, or trade names of their respective holders.

Published by Mark McCarthy.

Table of Contents

Chapter 1	Is this book for you?	3
Chapter 2	The Complete Guide to Your Backpack and other Planning	8
Chapter 3	Self-Care on the Camino	34
Chapter 4	Sarria to Portomarín	40
Chapter 5	Portomarín to Palas de Rei	67
Chapter 6	Palas de Rei to Arzúa	87
Chapter 7	Arzúa to Pedrouzo	113
Chapter 8	Pedrouzo to Santiago de Compostela	133
Chapter 9	Santiago de Compostela	143
Chapter 10	Background	161

Chapter 1 - Is this book for you?

Are you sort of interested in walking the Camino Francés but do not know much about it yet?

Well **yes**, then this book is for you. This guide will give you a straightforward introduction to walking the last 100km of the Camino. This book will take you through what it is likely to cost you both in terms of money and vacation days and how to minimise the cost. It will then lead you through how to prepare, what equipment is worth buying, what are the essentials to pack, what to leave at home and what you might consider bringing but is not essential. From the basics of packing the book will take you through where and how to start. The guide will lead you through the last 100km of the Camino, from village to village with maps of each village. These simple maps identify where the water fountains are, the cafés, the restaurants, the pharmacists and most importantly where the albergues (the pilgrim hostels) are located. I have put great effort into establishing accurate distances which includes the extra distance walked as you go up and the downhill. The distances given in this book are the most accurate available in any Camino guidebook. What initially motivated me to write this guidebook was frustration at the inaccurate distances and elevation charts in the current crop of guidebooks, which seemed to constantly under call both the distance and the steepness of ascents and descents. In addition, what further sets this guide apart from the other guides are the estimated walking times which accurately reflect the natural speed variations as you walk uphill and downhill. I give six estimates for each distance village to village which reflect accurately how long it will take based on your natural walking pace. I believe that the Camino is a fantastic experience for all and that all includes most of us who God never designed to be athletes. This guide is designed to include detailed GPS coordinates of all accommodation to allow you at the end of a hard day's walking to find your accommodation quickly and without stress. This guide provides details of cost, telephone number, GPS coordinates, address, email address and website (if available) for all albergues (pilgrim hostels). The guide will provide suggested daily itineraries (i.e., where to stop and stay) but I would ask that you try not to follow the suggested itineraries too closely as I strongly believe that in doing so you will miss out on making the Camino your own personal Camino. Also, some of the most interesting and welcoming albergues are to be found in the towns and villages in between the suggested stages. Try always to keep this one thought about the Camino in your mind and that is this the Camino is not about the destination, it is not about arriving it is instead about The Way. So, please take time and try and enjoy your Camino. At the beginning, it is hard not be sucked in to constantly moving quickly in a desire to get to Santiago but please try to resist and take as much time as you can spare to savour the experience.

Have you walked the Camino from Sarria before and are looking for an updated guidebook?

Again, **yes**, this guidebook is designed to give you accurate distances, maps which you do not need the internet available to look up and good estimates of how long it will take to walk to the next village. This guide will also provide you with detailed GPS coordinates not only for the next village but more usefully of every albergue on the route. So, when you arrive at your overnight stopping place you do not have to spend 10 minutes looking over the village map trying to work out where you are meant to be staying. In addition, this guide includes the latest cost, telephone number, email, and web address (if available) for all pilgrim accommodation along the way. When experienced as an eBook on a smartphone, this guidebook provides automatic links to phone numbers, GPS coordinates and web addresses.

You want recommendations for good or cheap places to stay?

Yes and **no**. Even in e-book it is difficult to keep an up to date set of recommendations. I have therefore kept recommendations for albergues out of this book. In general, I list the cheapest and biggest albergues first and the more expensive and smaller (and therefore generally better) albergues last. Also, if you want a list of recommended albergues please look at the Facebook page associated with this book:
www.facebook.com/SarriatoSantiago

Are you planning to walk the Camino Francés from León, Astorga, Ponferrada or O Cebreiro?

Then no, as I have written another guidebook which covers the Camino from León to Santiago called León to Santiago which is obviously bigger but only slightly more expensive. It is available in paperback and Kindle formats.

Are you planning to walk the whole of the Camino Francés?

Then no, while this guide will help you booking accommodation with last week of your Camino, you will need to purchase one of the many good guides with details of accommodation for the whole Camino.

Why a special version for the last 100km?

That is because it is the most popular starting point and approximately a third of all pilgrims on the Camino Francés start their pilgrimage from Sarria. The reason why so many pilgrims start from Sarria is that it is the last major starting point that allows a walking pilgrim to qualify for the official Compostela certificate. The fact that it only takes just under a week from Sarria makes it extremely attractive for those who are short of vacation. Starting in Sarria can be a great option for those who wish to arrive in Santiago for the feast of St James (which starts on the evening of July 24th and lasts till the evening of July 25th) but who are restricted on start date by other commitments such as exams. More on the Compostela and how to qualify for it later but suffice to say at this point the bishop of Santiago sets out minimum qualifying distance as being 100 km by foot or by horse and 200 km by bicycle.

Why choose this guidebook as opposed to the other good guidebooks?

1. This guidebook is focused on the needs of the pilgrims starting in Sarria including sections on how to get to Sarria and where to get any last-minute equipment in Sarria.
2. This guidebook provides 3D distances which includes the extra distance incurred by walking uphill and downhill to provide the most accurate distances available in any guidebook.

3. This guidebook provides the most accurate elevation maps available for the Camino which allows you to gauge the difficulty of each stage and plan accordingly.
4. This guidebook provides the most accurate estimated walking time available which recognizes that the speed at which people walk is affected by going up and down slopes. It can be extremely discouraging to attempt to maintain 4km/hr going up a steep slope. I believe it helps to recognize that you need to adjust your walking pace to steepness of the slope.
5. This guidebook provides more village maps than any other guidebook currently available for this stretch of the Camino. The village maps are useful for finding albergues that are not directly on the Camino as well as other amenities such as convenience shops and drinking fountains.
6. This guidebook is very competitively priced against similar guidebooks. It also combines packing and planning advice avoiding the need to buy an additional specialised book.
7. The Kindle version of this guide is one of only two guidebooks that automatically links to important websites.
8. If you are reading this on a smartphone or tablet or you have any other GPS enabled device, this is the only guidebook that provides GPS coordinates for every albergue.
9. The Kindle version of this guide provides clickable links to the email of each albergue that publishes their email address allowing you to email your booking or query.

Which version is best for you, paperback, or Kindle?

I currently sell four times as many paperbacks as I do Kindle versions. Most pilgrims want the security and "user friendliness" of a proper paperback. The Kindle version with its direct links to websites, email addresses and phone numbers is great for advance planning of your Camino. However, when on Camino most pilgrims appear to prefer using the paperback for ease of access. Many pilgrims like to take notes in their paperback edition and to keep as it a memento of their Camino. Personally, I prefer the Kindle edition for the ease of making phone calls to book ahead but I am in the minority.

Chapter 2 - The Complete Guide to Your Backpack and other Planning

When to walk?

The pilgrimage season from Sarria starts at Easter and lasts until the October school holidays. From November through March as few as 7 pilgrims a day set out from Sarria compared with the peak weeks in August when 500 pilgrims a day set off from Sarria. The largest number of pilgrims, however, set out from Sarria in the third week of July when pilgrim numbers on the Sarria leg swell to several thousand per day. This is because these pilgrims can arrive in Santiago for the evening of the Feast of St James (July 24th). This is a both a fantastic and terrible time to do your pilgrimage. Fantastic from the perspective of being able to celebrate the Feast of Saint James in Santiago, terrible from the fact that all albergues are fully booked and you will likely end up sleeping in one of the local schools which open up to absorb the huge numbers of additional pilgrims. Whichever week you choose to walk your Camino from Sarria to Santiago I hope you find the experience as moving and as fulfilling as I and so many others have and hope it gives you the taste to do one of the longer Caminos where you have so much more time to find peace, friendship and contentment on your Camino.

Which footwear to buy?

This is a subject of constant debate on the various Camino Facebook pages and online forums. I will try and layout the various opinions in as a balanced fashion as I can so that you can make your own mind up and choose the right footwear for you.

What is agreed by everyone is that you need to walk in your footwear before you go on Camino. The consensus is that you need at least two weeks of wearing your footwear for 3 hours per day at home. After this initial period, you can start your training walks with progressively increasing distance and weight in your backpack.

Time of the year will affect your choice as if you are walking anytime from November till April the route through Galicia can be very muddy which strongly favours the selection towards waterproof boots. In the summer, the heat pushes the choice more towards non-waterproof running shoes or walking sandals.

If you choose boots, then you must choose between leather or synthetic boots. The leather boots are tougher but are hotter and take several more weeks to walk in.

Please always select your footwear in a store where you can try on a wide variety of footwear. Remember if they feel right, they are likely to be right. If walking in the heat of the summer your feet will expand slightly during the day, so you may need to go one European (half a US/UK) size above your normal size.

If you are in anyway unsure on your feet, then this would favour boots with ankle support. If you struggle with the heat, then this would favour the choice of walking sandals with toe protection. Having walked with a fellow pilgrim who made a 4500km Camino in the summer, he strongly advocated walking sandals.

Personally, I have tried boots, walking shoes and walking sandals and I now take a combination of synthetic boots and walking sandals for summer Caminos and synthetic boots and crocs for winter Caminos. In the summer, I often switch to walking sandals for the last 4 or 5km to let my feet cool down a little. I have walked a 900km Camino with walking shoes which was a good compromise for most of the Camino but was not great on rocky paths and descents, so I have switched back to more robust synthetic boots. My parting piece of advice is to choose the footwear that feels right for you!

Which Backpack to buy?

Backpacks are like boots; you must at least try them on in a shop before buying them. Ordering them on the internet without having found out which feels most comfortable for you first is a false economy. If you are walking in the summer months you should be looking at a pack size of between 33 and 40 litres. Although some people can get by with a smaller pack size (even as small as 20 litres). These ultra-small packs not only make it very difficult to locate individual items but make it difficult every morning to repack your bag in a dark dorm room. Additionally, important features such as an offset mesh back and adjustable back length are not available on these ultra-small packs. When travelling from October till May it is advisable to bring a sleeping bag. Sleeping bags vary in packed size from about 7 litres to about 17 litres so you may need to be looking for a 40 to 55 litre pack for a winter Camino. There are plenty of good brands out on the market, so look to pay no more than about €100. After size and weight, one of the other important factors in your selection of a backpack is whether the backpack is height adjustable. An adjustable back height feature is important to get the majority of the weight resting on your hips. Especially for a summer Camino a backpack with an off-set mesh back that allows your back to breathe is highly desirable as you can lose significant amounts of water through you back and you may have to carry more water to compensate.

Personally, I have two packs, a Lowe Alpine 35:45 for the summer, which is super lite and has a great mesh back which I have been able to use as cabin luggage on several different low-cost airlines. For the winter I love my Osprey Atmos AG (Anti-Gravity feature) which is just super comfortable but is heavier and forces me to pay for hold luggage. Of the two I still prefer the heavier Osprey for sheer comfort. My final piece of advice on backpacks is to repeat my first piece of advice, that is try a variety of packs in a shop and go for the one that feels most comfortable.

How much should your pack weigh?

The rule of thumb is no more than 10% of your body weight. If you are an average woman this gives you 8kg (18lb) to play with of which about 1.5kg (3lb) will be taken up by your backpack. For young adults and those with smaller frames this rule gives you just 6kg (13lb) to play with. For those who do have little weight to play with, it may be worth going beyond €100 and investing in an ultra-light weight backpack from the likes of Deuter, Osprey or Lowe Alpine as this can give you up to another kilogram (2lb) to work with. Alternatively, it might be worth considering using one of the dedicated backpack transportation services.

Should I carry or ship my pack?

There are some people who think to be a "true pilgrim" one must always carry one's own backpack. To me the concept of trying to be a "true pilgrim" misses the point of pilgrimage in that pilgrimage is something God does for us not something we do for God. Pilgrimage is a special time for us to reflect on life and be at one with the world, whether you carry your pack or not is not critical to this. Having said that, I personally normally choose to carry my own pack as I really enjoy the freedom it gives me especially on the longer 800km+ Caminos. On the Sarria to Santiago route if I am travelling with a group, I usually encourage people to ship their pack and just carry a day pack. The reason I do this is that when travelling in a group it is advisable to pre-book accommodation in private albergues (municipal and parish albergues will generally not allow advance bookings) so you can keep the group together. Therefore, there is no need for flexibility. Additionally, for most people the first three days of pilgrimage are the physically the toughest and having your pack shipped can make an enormous difference. The cost of having your pack shipped on the Sarria to Santiago route is currently somewhere between 3 and 5 euros per day per bag or you can buy a package which costs from €20 for the whole trip.

How do I ship my pack?

There are several companies that ship packs on the Sarria to Santiago route. The feedback on all these companies is generally very good. The process is that you get labels to stick on each bag with your name, the name and the town of the albergue you are shipping from and most importantly the albergue and town you are shipping to. You will also get an envelope to put the money inside which you tie to the bag. If you are in a group and shipping more than one pack you only have to have prepare one envelope to cover all the bags, but each bag must have its own label. The evening before you must call the transportation company (don't worry if you don't speak any Spanish as they speak and understand basic English) to tell them that there are bags to collect from your albergue and where they are to be shipped to. The albergues have little or no control over the shipping companies so sometimes they are reluctant to get too involved in the process of shipping bags other than to provide the labels and an area in the reception to leave the bags to be shipped. However, some of the better albergues will provide a range of labels from different shipping companies to give you a choice, they will also help with change for the envelope, and some will even make the phone call to the transportation company for you. You do not have to stay in the albergue where you are having the bag shipped to. Some people have their packs shipped to one of the central albergues and then look around at a couple of albergues before deciding where to stay at. But obviously if you know where you are staying it is better to get your bags shipped directly there. There is generally a weight limit of 15kg on the packs but from personal observation the shipping companies seem not to enforce this rule. Some people take a dedicated bag between two people to save money.

CAMINO COMODO
caminocomodo.com +34 6 1775 4440
info@caminocomodo.com

PILBEO.COM
www.pilbeo.com +34 6 7064 8078
contact@pilbeo.com

CAMINOFÁCIL
caminofacil.net/en +34 6 1079 8138
contacto@caminofacil.net

CORREOS
www.elcaminoconcorreos.com/en/rucksack-transfer
+34 6 8344 0022 elcamino@correos.com

JACOTRANS
www.jacotrans.es +34 6 0604 9858
jacotransleon@gmail.com

Some of these companies offer a package rate for the whole journey. Currently the most competitive of these is the Spanish postal service (Correos) which offers a flat fee of €20 to ship your bag each day from Sarria to Santiago irrespective of how many days you take.

There is a further advantage to pre-booking bag shipping through Correos in that it allows you to enter all you overnight stops and print one luggage tag to cover the whole week. If you do choose this option, you may want to laminate the label or print it on waterproof paper.

What Not to Pack?

I have put this section first as it is more helpful to tell you what you don't need rather than what you do need.

- Tent. Why? There are no suitable sites for camping on the Sarria to Santiago leg.
- Stove. A stove with fuel is both heavy and a fire risk and one which you will not be permitted to use where there is any risk of forest fires.
- Sleeping bag. Well at least in the summer months, a sleeping bag liner together with extra clothes should be sufficient. Most but not all albergues will provide blankets if you ask. In the winter months if you are staying in albergues, a sleeping bag is a must. To minimise the weight, it is worth investing in a superlight (about 740g/26oz) sleeping bag which can be obtained for about €30 but it's probably not worth spending €110 on the ultralite (about 440g/16oz) sleeping bags.
- Cutlery. Anything made of steel even small items are heavy. If you are preparing your own food in an Albergue there will be cutlery there for you to use and if you are eating in a bar or restaurant, they will provide cutlery. Some people bring a polycarbonate spork with them, so they can enjoy a yoghurt or make their own sandwich at lunch time, but most pilgrims don't even bother with a spork. A spork is a combined spoon, fork and knife. They come in steel, aluminium, polycarbonate and titanium but the titanium version gives the best combination of strength and weight.
- Sat Nav system. Take a smartphone or tablet with GPS capability instead but make sure you download the apps and most importantly the maps for Spain before you set off as these are often huge.
- Full sized toiletries. Don't take any full-size toiletries, stick with the 100ml limit set by the airlines for cabin luggage. In the unlikely event that you run out; you can buy replacement toiletries at local convenience stores along the way. The extra cost of buying these in small

quantities is a price well worth paying to avoid the extra weight of full-sized containers.
- Separate shampoo and body wash. Buy a simple shampoo that you can use as body wash as well.
- Razor blades. Just buy, use and dispose of disposable razor blades from the local stores as and when you need them.
- Non-walking clothes. If you want some smart clothes for a few days stay in Santiago, you have a couple of choices. If you pass through Santiago on your way to Sarria you can leave a bag with all your smart clothes at Casa Ivar (www.casaivar.com/luggage-storage-in-santiago-de-compostela/index.html). Alternatively, you can post ahead some smart clothes to yourself for collection at the Santiago Post Office or at Casa Ivar. Thirdly and perhaps most simply use one of the luggage transfers services. Only carry what you are going to use each day.
- Spare shoes. Shoes are very heavy. You will need something for your feet as most albergue will ask you to leave your boots or walking shoes outside but something light such as crocs should be your only alternative footwear.
- A compass. The Camino is marked by yellow arrows along the entire route. It is entirely possible to walk the whole Camino without a guide nor a map nor a compass. Though as a guidebook writer I am hoping you will obviously see the advantages of using a guidebook. If you still feel the need for a compass remember there are many good compass apps, you can download to your smartphone.
- A camera. Modern smartphones provide superb quality photographs as well as high quality videos. There are numerous advantages of using your phone for taking photographs including ease of uploading and always being to hand, but the most important reason is to save weight.
- Cotton clothes. Cotton is a relatively heavy fabric when compared to modern synthetic material. It holds moisture against your skin rather than taking it away

from your skin. The only two natural fibres you should consider using are silk and merino wool. Otherwise, all your clothing should be fully synthetic. The main reason for this is weight but also synthetic materials are easier to clean and dry.
- A pillow. Virtually all albergues will provide a pillow. If no pillows are available just use some of your clothes.
- Makeup. Most people who carry makeup, end up not using it during the Camino, as they are just too physically tired to invest the time in putting on makeup. If you want some for the end of your Camino, do as I have suggested for smart clothes. i.e., send ahead to Santiago or more simply use one of the baggage transfer services.

What should you definitely pack?

- A Smartphone. These are versatile and useful, and everyone has one, so they are not the target for thieves they once were. Your smartphone will act as your watch, your alarm clock, your camera, your guidebook, your email and internet connection as well as your phone.
- A small battery power bank. Charging points are still scarce in most albergues. While you may not be making phone calls every day, remember your phone is also your camera and you will want to keep it with enough charge to take photographs along the way. If you are struggling with battery charge, airplane mode saves battery but allows you to use GPS and take photographs.
- One fleece. Even in the summer, there will be times you will need to keep warm.
- Sun Cream with a minimum of factor 15. You need to make sure you get into the habit of reapplying the sun cream at the end of every break and despite it's cost you will need to purchase more along the way and use even if you have developed a suntan.
- Deodorant. Keep the amount of deodorant you carry to a bare minimum again no more than 100ml and buy replacement deodorant along the way.

- Water containers to carry at least 2 litres (68 fluid ounces) of fluid in the heat of the summer. In the winter, you can reduce this to just half a litre (17 fluid ounces).
- 3 pairs of (anti-chafing) underwear.
- 3 pairs of walking socks preferably made from merino wool as merino wool kills off the bacteria which causes foot odour.
- 3 wicking (walking type) t-shirts. Most modern walking and running type t-shirts are designed so the fibres act as wicks which draw moisture away from your skin keeping your skin dry which is important on long strenuous walks.
- 2 pairs of full-length running tights or walking trousers (preferably ones which can be converted to shorts) and 1 pair of shorts or 2 pairs of shorts and 1 pair of trousers / running tights. Full length trousers / running tights are essential if the weather is poor or if you are vulnerable to sunburn.
- A large microfibre bath towel.
- Paper tissues or toilet roll, if you need to go to the toilet in the great outdoors.
- Wet wipes to clean your hands afterwards.
- Small plastic bags (poop bag style). To carry your used paper tissues, wet wipes or any other rubbish with you until you reach a bin.
- A poncho or lightweight raincoat with good waterproofing characteristics. The rain in Spain does not mainly fall on the plains; it mainly falls on Galicia! There is a reason why Galicia is beautifully green and lush so assume even in peak summer that it will rain heavily on at least one day.
- A raincover for your backpack. Most good backpacks will have an integrated raincover at the very top or very bottom of your backpack which you just pull out.
- A sun hat.
- A pumice stone to rub off dead skin and keep your feet supple.
- Ear plugs. You will be sleeping in dormitories. Many people snore when they sleep. Some snore very loudly. It

is therefore worth investing in good ear plugs. In terms of determining how good ear plugs are, you need to look for SNR number in Europe and the NRR number in North America. There are only very slight differences between these two rating systems and the higher the rating the better. You should be looking to buy plugs with a rating of 33 or above. Some suitable ear plugs are: the 3M E-A-Rsoft FX Earplugs, the Howard Leight MAX and the HEAROS Xtreme Protection.
- Barrier (baby) cream if you are prone to chaffing injuries.
- Compeed plasters or PodoPro felt pads (available via Ebay). These are the felt pads used by podiatrists. You can stick the pad to your foot with a cut out for the blister, so you can walk without putting any pressure on the blister itself. This will get you through the first 24 hours of a blister, after which time the blister can be drained.

Non-essentials you might want to pack?

- A Kindle in place of any paper books as a Kindle weighs less than even just one book and one charge will last your whole Camino.
- Extra underwear.
- A long sleeve wicking type walking t-shirt. You can always layer up with multiple t-shirts if you feel the cold at night.
- Walking sticks/poles. Most pilgrims use either walking sticks or a wooden staff, some even use a branch they find along the way. They are particularly helpful when going around muddy patches, going uphill and even more so going downhill. The stretch from Sarria to Santiago is very hilly but doesn't have the very steep descents that mandate the use of walking poles. In Winter and Spring, the paths particularly from Palas de Rei to Arzua can be very muddy and even partially flooded. This is where a pole or a stick is probably essential. In summer and early autumn, I have walked without poles, mainly to avoid the extortionate hold luggage fees (as most airlines and some countries including the UK explicitly prohibit carrying walking poles in cabin luggage). It is ultimately a question of personal taste as to whether you use walking

sticks or not but the consensus appears to be moving towards most people favouring the use of walking poles. If you do choose to use walking poles it is recommended to spend some time learning on how to use the poles effectively. There are some excellent YouTube videos which will help you get the most benefit from your walking sticks. When it comes to walking poles, the consensus is that anti-shock mechanisms add unnecessary weight to walking sticks and any benefits gained from going downhill with anti-shock are outweighed by the extra effort in going uphill with anti-shock. For cushioning, the better-quality poles come with cork handles or similar. The better poles also come with quick lock rather than twist tightening. In terms of weight there is a premium for lightweight with carbon fibre poles being the most expensive (expect to pay €70 upwards). Due to the extortionate cost of hold luggage, some people who travel with packs small enough to fit into cabin luggage (including my wife and myself) are now buying cheap walking poles (about €8 each pole) from Peregrinoteca in Sarria and then just ditching them at Santiago airport. Correos (the Spanish postal service) now offer a service at the airport where you can mail your walking sticks home, but this costs about €20.

- A micro-down ultra-light jacket or gilet (not required in the summer). This can double up as a very good pillow.
- A guidebook. Despite having a financial interest in encouraging you to purchase a guidebook, the reality is that you simply do not need a guidebook. You can simply follow the yellow arrows (flechas amarillas) all the way from Sarria without ever referring to a guidebook. Having said all that, a guidebook does make life easier. It helps you decide how far you want to walk each day. It helps you during the day in deciding whether to call it a day or to push on to the next village. It helps you decide which albergue you can afford and which albergue you are likely to prefer. It lets you phone or email ahead and ensure you have somewhere to sleep that night. It gives you background to where you are, and it helps you plan the

challenge ahead, knowing how steep and how long the hike to the next stop will take. Generally, it is a good idea to have a guidebook with you and I hope you choose this guidebook.
- A small LED torch. You can use your smartphone at night around the albergue but if you are doing any early morning walking, then a head torch is worth the extra weight required.
- Waterproof trousers. They are light and are probably worth packing but are not essential.
- A coarse mesh laundry bag to put your dirty washing in. This also facilitates sharing washing machines and tumble dryers with other pilgrims.

How to get to Sarria

- By train from Madrid there are four daytime services from Madrid Chamartín. The cost of your ticket to Sarria will cover getting the Cercanías (local Madrid suburban network) train from Madrid Airport to Chamartín. There is a railway station on the ground floor of Terminal T4. You will need either take the line C1 or C10 and there is only one direction as this is the start of the line. To get the free Cercanías ticket you will need to show your Madrid to Sarria ticket at the ticket booth. The trains run every 15 minutes or so and take 16 minutes. But... to be honest I often cheat and get a taxi which has a flat fee of €30 and takes 20 minutes. The cost of the tickets from Madrid to Sarria is about 30 euro for the daytime services.
- On the way back from Santiago to Madrid you can either get a fast train or a shuttle flight with either Ryainair, Vueling or Iberia.
- By train from Barcelona there is one daytime direct service from Barcelona Sants. The daytime services cost from 30 euro, takes up to 11 and half hours and picks up from Pamplona, Zaragoza, Burgos and Leon among other locations.
- For further details on train services in Spain contact Renfe (**www.renfe.com +34 9 1232 0320**).

Train timetable from Madrid

MADRID CHAMARTÍN	SARRIA
10:00	13:49
13:15	17:28
16:00	21:09
20:35	00:08

Train timetable from Barcelona

BARCELONA SANTS	SARRIA
09:00 (via Madrid)	17:28
09:30	21:09

- By coach from Santiago. It may sound strange to fly to Santiago to get the bus to Sarria and then to walk back to Santiago. However, this is one of the most popular routes to get to Sarria and makes the return journey home easier. There is one direct bus from Santiago to Sarria each day with Monbus. However, Monbus also offer a service to Lugo bus station and from there another Monbus bus to Sarria. The Monbus bus stops directly outside Santiago airport terminal. If you choose to visit Santiago first, then you can get the same bus from Santiago main bus station 15 minutes earlier. The bus costs about €11. For further details, contact Monbus (www.monbus.es/en).

Coach Timetable

As of January 2023, the current timetable is as follows:

Mondays to Fridays

SANTIAGO AIRPORT	ARRIVE LUGO	DEPART LUGO	SARRIA
07:15	08:50	10:30	11:09

11:15	direct	direct	13:01
17:15	18:30	18:35	19:15

Saturdays

SANTIAGO AIRPORT	ARRIVE LUGO	DEPART LUGO	SARRIA
11:15	direct	direct	13:06
15:15	16:50	17:30	18:10

Sundays

SANTAIGO AIRPORT	ARRIVE LUGO	DEPART LUGO	SARRIA
11:15	direct	direct	13:06
15:15	16:50	17:30	18:10

- By private hire direct from Santiago airport. This can be an expensive (about €130) option but if there are 3 or 4 of you this is affordable and gets you to Sarria and saves an additional overnight stay in Santiago. The journey takes about an hour and a half. There are several companies you can pre-book and it is definitely worth shopping around. Some of the many companies that offer pre-booking include:
    - Taxi Galicia.com (www.taxigalicia.com)
    - Xacotrans (www.xacotrans.com)
    - Taxi Peregrino.com (www.taxiperegrino.com)
    - Taxi Galicia.eu (www.taxigalicia.eu)
    - Taxi Peregrino.es (www.peregrinotaxi.es)
- By coach to Santiago from Oporto, Vigo and La Coruna via ALSA (www.alsa.es).

How much will it cost?

- On a very tight budget you can live on €33 per day which roughly breaks down to €12 for accommodation, €11 for your evening meal, €6.50 for lunch and €3.50 for

breakfast. However, this is a very tight budget, and most pilgrims tend to budget on about €38-€45 a day as a much more realistic figure. Santiago is significantly more expensive than being on the Camino. You should budget for about €60 a day as a minimum for Santiago itself.
- If you are staying in private accommodation, I would budget €60 per day for accommodation and €30 per day for other expenses.

How do you keep the cost down?

- Most of your money will be spent not on accommodation but on drinks and food and here just sticking to water which is free will save you significant amounts of money as well as being healthier. To improve the taste of the water, you can prepare your water bottles or bladder by placing them in the albergue' s fridge overnight.
- Most albergues also have a kitchen facility and this is by far the best way to save money, not only by preparing your own evening meal but also by preparing sandwiches to carry with you for the next day.
- When planning your Camino, it is important to remember that overnight stays at either end of your trip tend to be the most expensive. Therefore, it is important balance reducing the cost of travel with the cost of extra overnight stays. For example, overnight train journeys in sleepers maybe expensive but when balanced against an overnight stay in Madrid or Barcelona they often work out more cost effective as well as more fun. Equally, the cost of an extra overnight stay in Santiago and taking the bus may contribute to justifying the cost of getting a taxi directly to Sarria.
- If you are short of money, then you should always try and stay in the religious and parish run albergues as these tend to be donativo for both the accommodation and the evening meal. Donativo means donating and you are expected to pay what you can afford which means if you can't afford anything then you don't pay anything. This can be a real boost for pilgrims who otherwise would not be able to afford the pilgrimage but requires the rest of

us to be slightly more generous when staying in these albergues.

Cash

- Despite the contactless payment revolution underway, there are large sections of the Camino which are still cash only.
- Each cash withdrawal from an ATM brings a cost with it. To minimise these without having to carry all my cash with me, I typically withdraw €200 when I get below €50 cash.
- Typically, the best exchange rates come from specialist travel cards such as FairFX in Europe and Charles Schwab in the US.
- Many banks in Spain charge an additional fee to use their ATMs. Banks which generally do not charge include ABANCA, IberCaja and most Euro6000 network machines.
- Banks which charge €2 or less include BBVA, Sabadell and Bankia.
- The most expensive (€5+) ATMs to use include Santander and Telebanco.
- Watch out for "dynamic currency conversion" which is where you offered the choice of being charged in your home currency or euros. Stick with euros as your home bank's currency rate will tend to be better.

Tipping

- Unlike the USA, tipping is not mandatory. A tip is a way to say that you were very pleased with the food or service.
- Your tip does not usually go directly to the server but is pooled to be shared by all the staff at the end of the shift or the week.
- If you are paying by card, then tip in cash. If you tip by card there is a chance this will just end up in the owner's profit.
- In small bars and cafes tipping is unusual and most people just round up the bill to the nearest euro.
- In fancier restaurants, the average tip is in the 5% range compared to the UK where the average tip is just below 10%. If you are from the US, this may seem mean compared with the expected 20% to 30% tip. However, it is

worth remembering that all staff in Spain are paid a minimum wage which means they are not expected to make most of their income thru tips.
- In taxis, again tips are not expected, simply round up to the nearest euro or add an extra euro to the charge.

What is the Pilgrim Passport?

The Pilgrim Credential or the Pilgrim Passport as it is more commonly known is a foldable card that you buy at the start of your pilgrimage. The card is designed to be stamped along the way to show you have walked the way. It is also the proof when staying at Albergues that you are a genuine pilgrim (and not just a tourist trying to take advantage of the very cheap pilgrim accommodation). You can get stamps (sellos) for your pilgrim passport at all the albergues along the way as well as most of the churches and cafes. Albergues, cafés, restaurants and churches compete to produce the most attractive and interesting stamps and most pilgrims appear to enjoy collecting the stamps. The pilgrim passport is a great memento of your pilgrimage. The pilgrimage office in Santiago expects that pilgrims who are walking just the last 100km to collect two stamps per for each day, but while I have seen people refused a certificate for clearly flouting these rules, I am personally unaware of anyone being refused the official certificate of completion (the Compostela) because they missed a stamp on a particular day. My advice is to collect as many stamps as possible as the pilgrim passport is such a good memento.

Compostelas "vicare pro"

You can walk your Camino for someone who has passed or for someone who is unable to walk and is very ill due to a life limiting illness. If you wish to do this, please tell the pilgrim office when you hand in your pilgrim passport. The Compostela is still issued in your name but is annotated "vicare pro" followed by the name of the person. "Vicare pro" means "in the place of".

Example Pilgrim Passport

Example Compostela Certificate of Completion

Capitulum hujus Almae Apostolicae et Metropolitanae Ecclesiae Compostellanae sigilli Altaris Beati Jacobi Apostoli custos, ut omnibus Fidelibus et Peregrinis ex toto terrarum Orbe, devotionis affectu vel voti causa, ad limina Apostoli Nostri Hispaniarum Patroni ac Tutelaris SANCTI JACOBI convenientibus, authenticas visitationis litteras expediat, omnibus et singulis praesentes inspecturis, notum facit: Dnum.

Maraim McCarthy

hoc sacratissimum Templum perfecto utique pedibus sive equitando itinere postrema centum millia metrorum, birota vero ducentorum, pietatis causa devote visitasse. In quorum fidem praesentes litteras, sigillo ejusdem Sanctae Ecclesiae munitas, ei confero.

Datum Compostellae die 24 mensis Iulii anno Dni 2014

Segundo L. Pérez López
Deán de la S.A.M.I. Catedral de Santiago

Where do you get a Pilgrim Passport from?

Online from the Camino Forum
www.santiagodecompostela.me/products/official-pilgrim-credencial-pilgrim-passport-from-the-pilgrims-office-in-santiago

This is a very convenient and quick option as Ivar who runs the forum mails them out very quickly and at a reasonable price. This is my preferred option.

Online from APOC (American Pilgrims on the Camino)
americanpilgrims.org/request-a-credential

There is some very good information about collecting stamps (sellos) on this request page, so it is worth a look even if you don't order from APOC.

From the Irish Friends of Saint James
Either Online.
www.caminosociety.com/shop
OR....
In person from the sacristy of the Church of St James, James Street, Dublin 8 (53.34338 -6.28831) (Monday to Friday 10:00 am to 12:00 pm). The church of St James is opposite the world-famous St James's Gate Guinness brewery. The brewery gets its name from the medieval western gate into Dublin which was the traditional starting point of Irish pilgrimages to Santiago. Apparently after getting your Irish pilgrim's passport, you can visit the brewery and get your first stamp from the Guinness brewery itself. The cost of the Irish pilgrim passport is 10 euro which seems expensive, but this money is used to help fund the Irish Friends of St James.

In Sarria
The pilgrim passport can be purchased from the church of Santa Mariña, Rúa de Maior (open 11 am till 1 pm and 6 pm till 9 pm except Mondays when they are open 7 pm till 8 pm) (42.77745, -7.44146) or from the monastery of the Magdalena, Avenida de la Merced, 60 (open 10 am till 1 pm and from 4 pm till 7 pm) (42.77905, -7.42112) or from the Albergue Credencial (42.77497, -7.4091).

Do you really have to get up at 6 am in the morning?

In the summer months, it is generally too hot to walk between the hours of 1 pm and 7 pm and as a consequence you really need to get all your walking done in the morning. This requires that you set your alarm for about 5:30 and be out walking by 6am. Most cafés along the Camino open especially early to cater for pilgrims and many pilgrims including myself aim to get an hour's walking in before stopping for breakfast. Getting up at 5:30 means you need to be getting to bed by about 9 pm. This may sound unusual, but your body needs as much rest as possible and you will adjust to this schedule very quickly. In the non-summer months, I would strongly advise against walking in the early morning dark. The biggest cause of death on the Camino is from road traffic accidents and it is simply not worth the risk of any road walking while it is still dark.

How to use the GPS Coordinates

I give the GPS coordinates in decimal degrees as this format can be more easily used in GPS applications such as MAPS.ME, Google Maps or Google Earth. If you have a smartphone or tablet to read this book you will be able to click on the decimal GPS coordinates and this should open Google Maps in a web browser on your device and should identify a walking route from your current location to GPS coordinates you clicked.

Finding the way - waymarks and yellow arrows

The route is very well waymarked with a combination of granite columns (mojones) which point the way. These are put in place by the local authorities. Often there are yellow arrows painted on the ground, trees, walls, in fact anywhere obvious, to complement the mojones. The yellow arrows are painted by volunteers from local pilgrim associations. Regrettably at times bars and restaurants also paint unofficial yellow arrows to lead pilgrims to their establishment.

Emergency Numbers

112 is the general Emergency Number in Europe. They will answer very quickly even if there is no credit on your phone. Explain slowly

and clearly that you need to speak to an operator in English if that is the case. It will help if you work out your location from the guidebook.

Victims of Crime

There is a dedicated English-language telephone number for victims of crimes who wish to make a police report but do not speak Spanish. The number is (+34) 902 102 112. It operates from 9am to 9pm daily.

Flora and Fauna on the Camino

Along the route you will see many species of trees and wildflowers. Species of trees include lemon and philadelphus, oak, chestnut, and pine. You will also see the predominant and invasive eucalyptus – allegedly imported from Australia early in the last century in exchange for Merino sheep. Wildflowers include orchids, lilies, white campion, cow parsley, vetch, and foxgloves ... to name but a few. Along the way you will also see many vegetable gardens and walk through lush tree tunnels.

Estimated walking times

One of the constant frustrations I had during my first Camino was with the distances and the estimated walking times in the current crop of guidebooks. These distances and estimated walking times seem to bear very little similarity to my experience. An ever-present topic of conversation among fellow pilgrims was the "Camino kilometre" which varied in length somewhere between 1.1km and 1.9km. As for the estimated walking times, it was clear that the person who wrote the guidebook I used when I made my first Camino was extremely fit or extremely bad at recording times accurately. In this guide, I want to give you as the reader a realistic expectation of how much time each stretch will take, so that you can make sensible decisions about whether to push on to the next village or stay where you are. I believe that the Camino is best experienced at the pace that your body dictates. I have put a lot of effort into the estimated timings, but they are purely there as an aid to deciding about where you stop for the evening or where you stop for brunch or lunch. In an attempt to give you good ballpark estimates for each stage, I give 3 estimated timings which are based on three walking speeds. The fastest time is based on a what is called a "preferred walking speed" of 5.3 km/hr walking speed, which is roughly the preferred walking speed of a fit person with no backpack on the flat ("preferred walking speed" - research shows that although most people can walk at speeds of up to 7.5 km/hr, we naturally walk at a pace that minimise the amount of energy used for the distance covered and this is in the region of 4.1 to 5.3 km/hr when not encumbered down by a backpack). The slowest time is 3.9km/hr and is based upon someone who is not super fit and is carrying a backpack on the flat. The middle timing is based on a preferred walking speed of 4.6km/hr on the flat and is roughly equivalent to a normal fit person carrying a backpack on the flat. The timing considers the total 3D distance travelled and the effect on walking speed of going up and downhill. (For more than 100 years, hikers have relied on Naismith's rule to estimate walking times when the terrain goes up and down. Naismith's rule was improved upon and made into Tobler's rule, but it wasn't until 2012 when two Japanese researchers, Yasuhisa Kondo and Yoichi Seino, decided to develop their own rule from scratch using the GPS data from real life hikes that there has been an evidence-based calculation available. With Kondo and Seino's calculation it is possible to estimate hiking times over terrain where the slope is constantly changing. Currently this is the best method available and has formed the basis for the estimates included in this guide).

Alternative Stages

The most common strategy for splitting Sarria to Santiago in to six days is to split the long third day from Palas de Rei to Arzua in to two short days by overnighting in Melide.

An alternative split might look something like:
Sarria to Vilachá	19.8 km
Vilachá to Lestedo	21.0 km
Lestedo to Melide	18.8 km
Melide to Arzúa	14.2 km
Arzúa to Pedrouzo	20.4 km
Pedrouzo to Santiago	19.6 km

For a seven-day split I suggest the following:
Sarria to Mercadoiro	16.8 km
Mercadoiro to Ventas de Narón	17.7 km
Ventas de Narón to San Xulián do Camiño	14.6 km
San Xulián do Camiño to Boente	16.4 km
Boente to A Calle	16.3 km
A Calle to Amenal	14.9 km
Amenal to Santiago	17.0 km

For a ten-day split I suggest the following:
Sarria to Morgade	12.0 km
Morgade to Portomarín	9.6 km
Portomarín to Ventas de Narón	12.9 km
Ventas de Narón to Palas de Rei	11.2 km
Palas de Rei to Melide	14.0 km
Melide to Arzúa	14.2 km
Arzúa to Salceda	11.3 km
Salceda to Pedrouzo	9.1 km
Pedrouzo to Lavacolla	9.6 km
Lavacolla to Santiago	10.0 km

For those who struggle with such distances I have prepared an 18-stage plan which is available on the Camino Forum. You will need to register (which is free) to download (which is also free). The plan is at:

🕸 www.caminodesantiago.me/community/resources/sarria-to-santiago-in-very-short-stages.627/

Useful Stores on the Camino

Sarria

Peregrinoteca
- Calle Benigno Quiroga, 16 - Bajo 27600 Sarria (Lugo)
- 42.77678, -7.4128
- ☏ +34 9 8253 0190
- www.peregrinoteca.com/tienda/

Palas de Rei

Suseia Pilgrim Store
- Travesía de la Iglesia, N.º 7
- 42.87315, -7.86878
- ☏ +34 6 3606 8526

Santiago

Decathlon City
- Rúa da República de El Salvador, 31- 33,
- 42.87443, -8.54864
- ☏ +34 9 8159 4022

Decathlon
- Calle Polonia Nº2 15707 (414) SANTIAGO
- 42.90244, -8.5102
- ☏ +34 9 8189 7516

El Corte Inglés
- Rúa do Restollal, 50 15702 Santiago de Compostela, A Coruña
- 42.8625, -8.54329
- ☏ +34 9 8152 7200

Chapter 3 - Self-Care on the Camino

Keeping your fluid intake up

You will lose substantially larger amounts of water than you are used to when walking particularly in the summer. When you lose water to perspiration you also lose two very important salts Sodium Chloride and Potassium Chloride. If either your Potassium or Sodium levels drop too far you will very suddenly feel light headed, you may well faint and if you don't restore your salt levels to normal it can be life threatening especially in the intense heat, so this small section is important. The recommendation is that in the summer you carry at least 2 litres of drinking water with you at all times. You should replenish your water bottles at every opportunity. It is advisable to always carry rehydration salts with you. Rehydration salts are sold as diarrhoea rehydration powder. These rehydration salts are expensive, but I would encourage you to carry them if not for yourself then for other pilgrims who may become dehydrated. You can buy soft drinks which have the correct balance of rehydration salts, water and sugar. Coca-Cola market such a product called Aquarius which is sold widely on the Camino. It comes in just two flavours lemon and orange and is not as tasty as the carbonated drinks but is much better for you when you are walking. There are supermarket equivalents which are very similar but much cheaper and if you find they suit you, it is worth buying a couple of litres in the local supermarket in the evening for the next day. One word of caution is that Aquarius contains sugar and therefore is not suitable if you are diabetic. Alternatively, you can drink water for free. If there are no drinking taps available, there is a tradition that anyone who lives on the Camino will always provide water to a thirsty pilgrim. Please remember this is only a tradition and people who live on the Camino have every right to refuse. None the less, this is a tradition which in my experience is observed and the good people who live on the Camino are often quite willing to fill your water bottle. It is likely you will need to increase your use of table salt on your food to balance the amount of sodium you lose through perspiration.

This is needed while you are walking such large distances in the heat, but it is important to remember when you get home that additional table salt in your normal diet is bad for your blood pressure. To keep your Potassium levels up the easiest options are bananas, potatoes, beans, mushrooms, pears, fish and yoghurt.

Public water taps come in three types. The safest type is those which have chlorinated water from the town's drinking water supply (aqua potable), the second type is untreated drinking water (fuente natural) which you drink at your own risk, the third (aqua no potable) is guaranteed to be unsafe for drinking.

There are three choices when it comes to carrying water. Firstly, are the specialised water bladders. Even the high-quality water bladders from the likes of Osprey and Camelbak can be purchased on the internet for around €25. If you are going to invest in a water bladder, then it is worth paying for a good quality bladder. A good quality bladder is one that has high quality seams that have been well tested against leaks and that have an in-built flat shape that keeps the water from pooling at the bottom of your backpack. While generally the lower is better when it comes to weight, it is even better that weight is as close to your spine as possible which the shaped bladders ensure. In addition, the shaped bladders minimise any slopping of the water which will have a small but persistent energy zapping effect. Finally, on water bladders, the better-quality bladders are made from anti-microbial materials which will help prevent any nasty bugs finding a home in the water bladder.

The second alternative is the good quality 1 litre lightweight aluminium water cans which can be purchased for about €5 on the internet. These are not quite as handy as the water bladders but pulling out and putting back a fellow pilgrim's water can in their backpack pockets is an extremely social activity that can be the start of a great conversation with a fellow pilgrim and sometimes it can be the start of lifelong friendship.

The third alternative is to simply re-use the plastic water bottles you purchase the water in. They are very light and will normally last a few days or even a week or two. Again, this has the advantage of requiring you to ask a fellow pilgrim for help if you don't want to stop and take your backpack off.

Feet Care on the Camino

Unless you are a regular walker, on a 100km walk you will develop problems with your feet despite the best boots and the best socks available. As with most things prevention of blisters is much better than cure. Blisters are caused by friction between your sock and your skin. The choice of sock is therefore important. Research has shown that twin layer socks help reduce the incidence of blisters. Most good walking socks have twin layers on the points most likely to rub.

The second risk factor for the friction that causes blisters is moisture, again choosing modern walking socks that are designed to wick moisture away from the skin on your foot is a wise investment. You can also help reduce the risk of blisters by regularly taking your boots or shoes off, changing your socks and letting your feet cool down and dry off.

Finally keep the skin of your feet supple by rubbing off the hard dead skin with a pumice stone. This will allow the skin of your feet to be more flexible and thereby avoid the friction which causes blisters. Many pilgrims also recommend rubbing Vaseline into your feet each morning to reduce friction and thereby blisters.

In terms of treating blisters, research shows that draining blisters works better than padding them. Draining can be achieved by a method called "threading" or by cutting a hole in the blister. "Threading" is where you thread a needle with cotton and sow the cotton through your blister in order to drain the blister. The thread is left in overnight to ensure that the blister remains drained. However, threading involves significant risk of serious infection even if you apply generous amounts of iodine to the needle, the thread and your foot. It is difficult to do to your own feet and it is painful, and I must confess I have done it to myself in the past. However, my very strong recommendation if at all possible is to pay out the €30 consult fee and get a professional to look after your feet. I was extremely lucky on my first Camino that at the point where my feet were so bad that I was at my lowest point on my whole Camino and felt I could go no further that I was joined at the table where I was having lunch by an Irish podiatrist who was a complete stranger. This fellow pilgrim kindly gave me a free consult, patched me up and taught me what I needed to get my feet back in action after two days of rest. Rather than rely on just luck and partly as an expression of gratitude to my podiatric benefactor I am including a list of podiatrists along the way.

(A side note that when buying hiking socks buy the best you can afford, generally only buy hiking socks which are specific for each foot i.e., they are marked with an L and an R)

List of Podiatrists from Sarria to Santiago

Sarria

Clínica Podologica Alvarez
- Rúa Diego Pazos, 16
- 42.77894, -7.41181   ☏ +34 9 8253 5153

Podologo Marta Perez
- Rúa Calvo Sotelo, 68
- 42.78091, -7.41438   ☏ +34 9 8253 4153

Portomarín

Clinica del Pie
- Calle Diputación 2, Mercado Municipal L9
- 42.80789, -7.61617   ☏ +34 6 4445 7966

Palas de Rei

Pampin Negro
- Avda. de Compostela, 29 Bajo
- 42.8727, -7.86933   ☏ +34 9 8238 0121
- ☏ +34 6 3924 8332

Santiago

Clínica Podologica Federico Peñamaría
- Rúa de Ramón Cabanillas, 6
- 42.87327, -8.54990   ☏ +34 9 8159 8808

Saleta Becerra Noal
- Rúa da República de el Salvador, 28
- 42.874545, -8.548369   ☏ +34 9 8157 2388

Clínica Del Pie Sanjurjo
- Rúa de Frei Rosendo Salvado, 10
- 42.87371, -8.55033   ☏ +34 9 8159 4020

Clínica do Pé Óliver Regueiro
- Rúa De Madrid, 3 Bajo 2 Fontiñas - Frente A área Central
- 42.881385, -8.528218   ☏ +34 9 8159 3918

Clínica do Pé, Patricia Seoane Iglesias
- Rúa de Montero Ríos, 28
- 42.87565, -8.54705 ☏ +34 9 8159 3918

Clínica Riosan Fisioterapia & Podología
- Avenida da Mestra Victoria Míguez, 43
- 42.46968, -8.57368 ☏ +34 9 8152 2926

Podóloga Marina Porto Paredes
- Galeras, 9 Bajo
- 42.88291, -8.54877 ☏ +34 8 8103 1132
- www.podologiamarinaporto.es

Clínica do Pe Manuel Tojo
- Calle Doutor Teixeiro 28, 1º
- 42.87408, -8.54572 ☏ +34 8 8197 4412
- ☏ +34 6 8564 7175
- www.manueltojopodologo.es

Secundino Coto Podólogo
- Montero Ríos, 33 2º C
- 42.87540, -8.54780 ☏ +34 8 8197 7481
- ☏ +34 6 4927 9076
- www.secundinocotopodologo.es

Cepeda Clinica Podoloxica
- San Paio de Antealtares, 6 Baixo
- 42.88086, -8.54286 ☏ +34 9 8158 5758

Please note that this is the most central of the podiatrists and is in the road parallel and to the back of the Last Stamp.

Clínica Del Pie Mª Jose Fernandez
- Xeneral Pardiñas, 5 1º B
- 42.87603, -8.54614 ☏ +34 9 8193 7565

Clínica Podoloxica Galastur
- Avenida de Lugo, 7 Baixo
- 42.87199, -8.54397 ☏ +34 8 8195 9183

Chapter 4 - Sarria to Portomarín

Waypoint Summary Sarria to Portomarín

From	Waypoint	Decimal GPS	Distance	3.9 km/hr	4.6 km/hr	5.3 km/hr
Sarria	Vilei (Barbadelo)	42.76897 -7.44426	3.7km	1hrs 12mins	1hrs 1mins	0hrs 53mins
Vilei (Barbadelo)	Barbadelo	42.76784 -7.45235	1.0km	0hrs 19mins	0hrs 16mins	0hrs 14mins
Barbadelo	Rente	42.76810 -7.45900	0.7km	0hrs 13mins	0hrs 11mins	0hrs 10mins
Rente	A Serra	42.77099 -7.46704	0.7km	0hrs 15mins	0hrs 12mins	0hrs 11mins
A Serra	Peruscallo	42.78059 -7.49346	3.1km	0hrs 56mins	0hrs 47mins	0hrs 41mins
Peruscallo	Morgade	42.78218 -7.52120	2.8km	0hrs 51mins	0hrs 43mins	0hrs 37mins
Morgade	Ferreiros	42.78364 -7.53266	1.4km	0hrs 25mins	0hrs 21mins	0hrs 18mins
Ferreiros	Mirallos	42.78380 -7.53627	0.3km	0hrs 5mins	0hrs 4mins	0hrs 3mins
Mirallos	Pena	42.78541 -7.54262	0.5km	0hrs 9mins	0hrs 8mins	0hrs 7mins
Pena	As Rozas	42.78402 -7.54974	0.7km	0hrs 13mins	0hrs 11mins	0hrs 9mins
As Rozas	Mercadoiro	42.78867 -7.56871	1.8km	0hrs 31mins	0hrs 26mins	0hrs 23mins
Mercadoiro	A Parrocha	42.79401 -7.58755	1.7km	0hrs 30mins	0hrs 25mins	0hrs 22mins
A Parrocha	Vilachá	42.79558 -7.60349	1.3km	0hrs 22mins	0hrs 18mins	0hrs 16mins
Vilachá	Portomarín	42.80457 -7.61655	1.8km	0hrs 31mins	0hrs 26mins	0hrs 23mins
Sarria	Portomarín	42.80457 -7.61655	21.6km	6hrs 37mins	5hrs 37mins	4hrs 52mins

Sarria to Portomarín
Elevation Chart

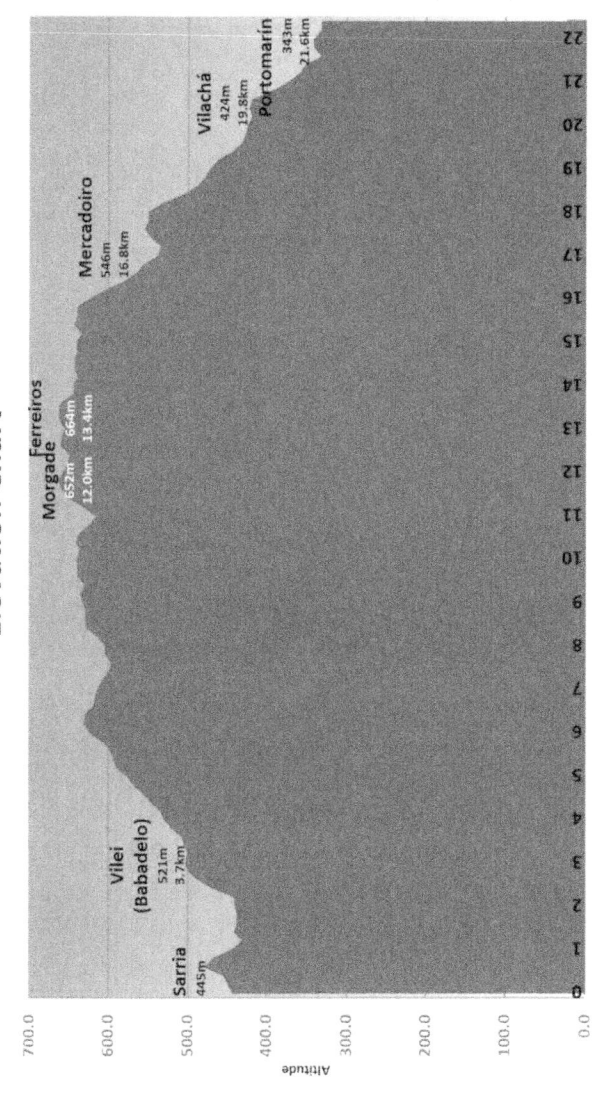

- Sarria 445m
- Vilei (Babadelo) 521m 3.7km
- Morgade 652m 12.0km
- Ferreiros 664m 13.4km
- Mercadoiro 546m 16.8km
- Vilachá 424m 19.8km
- Portomarín 343m 21.6km

42

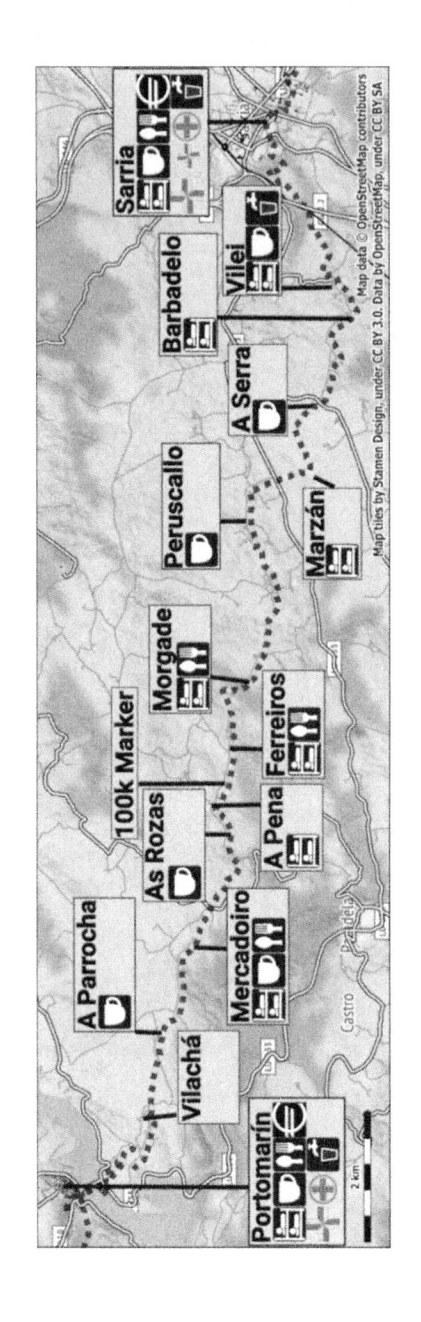

Notes about Today's Stage

The first part of your first day involves a climb of about 200m over about 5km. This is a moderate climb, and you may want to take a break after the first 4km in Vilei (Barbadelo). This is also an ideal opportunity for a morning comfort break before starting the relatively long stretch to Morgade. Remember most albergues will also act as a cafe/bar if there are no dedicated cafe/bars. After Vilei (Barbadelo), you pass by Barbadelo itself about 1km further on. Although there are hamlets on the way, it is another 7km to the next village Morgade. The good news is there is a moderate amount of shade along the route which eases the strain of the climb on a hot day. Morgade is the most popular stop for lunch. After Morgade you will have completed the main climb and the rest of the day is physically less demanding but note that the descent into Portomarín is steep which will slow you down. After Morgade you will pass through Ferreiros which is just before the official 100km marker and offers a good alternative lunch stop to Morgade. After Ferreiros you pass through the tiny hamlet of A Pena and thence to Mercadoiro which I find provides a very pleasant afternoon break. After Mercadoiro you will pass through the tiny hamlet of A Parrocha and finally Vilachá which is less than 2 km from Portomarín.

Without prior training, today, although a relatively short stage, still involves about 7 hours of walking due to the moderately steep climb and descent.

At certain points in Galicia including the descent into Porto Portomarín, you will be faced with the option of following two sets of the stone way markers (called mojones in Spanish). One set of markers will carry the distance to Santiago Cathedral and the other set of markers will just say "C. Complementario" which stands for Camino Complementario which means complementary or alternative route. The "C. Complementario" route is always slightly longer but is sometimes the recommended route as it is generally a more pleasant route.

Pilgrims now have three choices for the final descent towards Portomarín. The middle route is the "official" measured route but contains at one point a treacherous descent. The right route is the shortest route but is extremely steep and brings with it the risk of blisters due to the steepness of the descent. The left route adds about 400 metres, and the last few hundred metres are a bit rocky and ugly but is the easiest and recommended route.

The final walk into Portomarín is beautiful and takes you across the Belesar dam. As you cross you may be able to see on your left some of the remains of the original village which was flooded with the creation of the dam. The entrance into Portomarín itself is very steep but also very pretty as the archway, the church and several other buildings were relocated stone by stone when Portomarín was relocated as part of the creation of the dam.

Sarria

113.8km to Santiago. 3.7km to Vilei. Altitude 443m. Local Facilities= CAFE/BAR, RESTAURANT, ATM, HOTEL OR GUEST HOUSE TYPE ACCOMMODATION, PHARMACY, MEDICAL CENTRE, GROCERY STORE. GPS: 42.77718, -7.41378

Map of Sarria

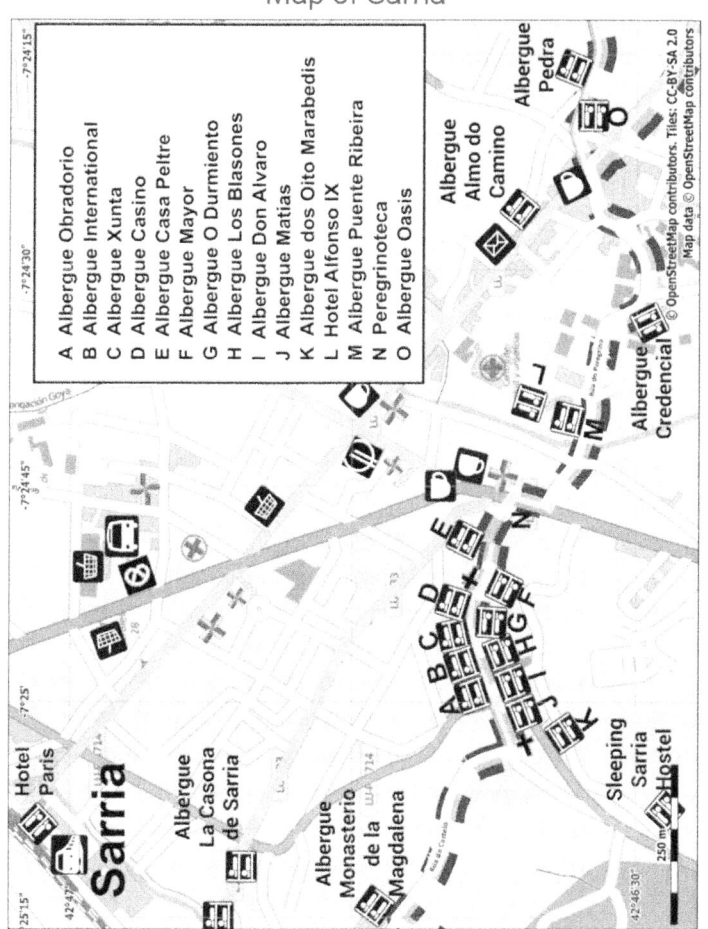

A Albergue Obradorio
B Albergue International
C Albergue Xunta
D Albergue Casino
E Albergue Casa Peltre
F Albergue Mayor
G Albergue O Durmiento
H Albergue Los Blasones
I Albergue Don Alvaro
J Albergue Matias
K Hotel Alfonso IX
L Albergue dos Oito Marabedis
M Albergue Puente Ribeira
N Peregrinoteca
O Albergue Oasis

Background on Sarria

Sarria probably gets its name from the pre-Roman Seurros tribe that is credited with the founding of the town. However, the town as we now know it had its foundation as a Jacobean (Camino) town in the 12th century when it was re-founded as Vilanova de Sarria (Sarria New Town) by King Alfonso IX of Leon (1171-1230). By coincidence Alfonso IX died in Sarria whilst on pilgrimage to Santiago to give thanks for the capture of Merida from the Moors. It was the death of Alfonso IX in Sarria that marked the creation of the country we now know as Spain for his son Ferdinand, who was already King of Castile through marriage, thus became King of the new combined kingdom of Castile and Leon.

The heart of Sarria is Rúa Mayor in the old town where most of the albergues and restaurants are to be found. Here too is the 19th century church of Santa Marina with its charming pilgrim mural on the outside wall. There is a good choice of restaurants including an authentic Italian run by Italians. If in season the Padron Peppers (green peppers grilled or fried in olive oil well seasoned with sea salt) is an absolute delight. The sharpness of the peppers depends on the time within the season, with early season peppers being sweeter and late season peppers carrying more of a punch. There is of course as with everywhere the delicious octopus, but I think this is a delicacy best experienced in the specialist pulperias in Melide. The temptation with so much great fish and seafood is to miss out on the local meat which is also excellent as most of this part of Galicia is dedicated to cattle farming (mainly for dairy but with some great beef as well).

On your exit from Sarria, you will climb up Rúa Maior in the old town. You need to turn first right just after the Italian restaurant. Follow the road until you see the Monastario of Magdalena in front of you. To follow the Camino, turn sharp left here. However, Monastario of Magdalena dates from the 13th century. The monastery was founded by two Italian pilgrims originally as a pilgrim hostel and it is now once again acting as an albergue. It is well worth the 20-metre detour to visit even if it is just to get your first passport stamp of the day.

After turning left, you head downhill for about 250 metres, then turn right and carry on the road for about 200 metres before turning left and crossing a small stone bridge. Please note that the railway line that you cross, although not busy, is still in use so you must look both ways before crossing. The climb up to Vilei is probably the steepest climb of the day so please don't be discouraged if it feels really tough.

Pilgrim Accommodation Sarria

Albergue Xunta
- Rúa Mayor, 57
- 42.77748, -7.414881
- +34 6 6039 6813

Min Cost= €8, No of Beds = 41, Facilities= KITCHEN, WASHING MACHINE, TUMBLE DRYER
Opening Times: 13:00 till 22:00. February 4 till December 19

Albergue Alma del Camino
- Rúa de Calvo Sotelo, 199
- 42.77641, -7.40742
- +34 6 2982 2036
- sarria@almadocamino.com
- www.almadelcamino.com

Min Cost= €12, No of Beds = 100, Facilities= KITCHEN, WASHING MACHINE, TUMBLE DRYER, WIFI
Opening Times: 11:30 till 23:00 February 15 till December 15
- www.booking.com/hotel/es/albergue-alma-do-camino.html

Albergue Puente Ribeira
- Rúa do Peregrino, 23
- 42.77584, -7.41161
- +34 9 8287 6789
- +34 6 9817 5619
- info@alberguepuenteribeira.com
- www.alberguepuenteribeira.com

Min Cost= €10, No of Beds = 50, Facilities= WASHING MACHINE, TUMBLE DRYER, WIFI, PRIVATE ROOMS AVAILABLE
Opening Times: 11:00 till 23:00 March 1 till October 31
- www.booking.com/hotel/es/albergue-puente-ribeira.html

Albergue Obradorio
- Rúa Mayor, 49
- 42.77741, -7.415545
- +34 9 8253 2442
- +34 6 4720 9267

Min Cost= €10, No of Beds = 38, Facilities= WASHING MACHINE, TUMBLE DRYER, WIFI
Opening Times: 11:00 till 23:00 Holy Week till October 31
- www.booking.com/hotel/es/obradoiro-sarria.es.html

Albergue Don Alvaro
- Rúa Mayor, 10
- +34 9 8253 1592
- info@alberguedonalvaro.com
- www.alberguedonalvaro.com
- 42.7771, -7.41667
- +34 6 8646 8803

Min Cost= €15, No of Beds = 40, Facilities= KITCHEN
Opening Times: 12:00 till 23:00. Open all year.
www.booking.com/hotel/es/albergue-casa-don-alvaro-sarria.html

Albergue Matías
- Rúa Mayor, 4
- +34 6 8324 3335
- info@matiaslocanda.es
- 42.77691, -7.4172
- +34 9 8288 6112
- matiaslocanda.es

Min Cost= €10, No of Beds = 32, Facilities= WASHING MACHINE, TUMBLE DRYER, WIFI, PRIVATE ROOMS AVAILABLE
Opening Times: 11:00 till 22:30. Open all year.
www.booking.com/hotel/es/albergue-en-sarria-matias-locanda.html

Albergue Credencial
- Rúa do Peregrino, 50
- +34 9 8287 6455
- alberguecredencial@gmail.com
- www.alberguecredencial.es
- 42.77497, -7.4091

Min Cost= €10, No of Beds = 28, Facilities= WASHING MACHINE, TUMBLE DRYER, WIFI
Opening Times: 09:30 till 23:30. Open all year.
www.booking.com/hotel/es/albergue-credencial.html

Albergue A Pedra
- Camino Vigo, 19
- +34 9 8253 0130
- info@alberguepedra.com
- 42.77640, -7.40606
- +34 6 5251 7199
- www.alberguepedra.com

Min Cost= €15, No of Beds = 15, Facilities= KITCHEN, WASHING MACHINE, TUMBLE DRYER, WIFI, PRIVATE ROOMS AVAILABLE
Opening Times: 11:00 till 23:00 March 1 till November 30
www.booking.com/hotel/es/albergue-a-pedra.html

Albergue Monasterio de la Magdalena
- Avenida de la Merced, 60
- +34 9 8253 3568
- 42.77905, -7.42113
- +34 8 1568 8521

✉ sarria@alberguesdelcamino.com
🌐 www.alberguesdelcamino.com
Min Cost: €10, No of Beds = 100, Facilities= KITCHEN, WASHING MACHINE, WIFI
🌐 www.booking.com/hotel/es/albergue-monasterio-de-la-magdalena.html

Albergue Internacional
- 📍 Calle Mayor, 57
- 📍 42.78082, -7.41414
- ☎ +34 9 8253 5109
- ✉ info@albergueinternacionalsarria.es
- 🌐 www.albergueinternacionalsarria.es

Min Cost= €10, No of Beds = 43, Facilities= WASHING MACHINE, PRIVATE, ROOMS AVAILABLE
Opening Times: 12:00 till 23:00 January 1 till October 31
🌐 www.booking.com/hotel/es/albergue-internacional.html

Albergue Los Blasones
- 📍 Calle Mayor, 31
- 📍 42.77746, -7.41603
- ☎ +34 6 0051 2565
- ✉ albergue@losblasones.com
- 🌐 www.alberguelosblasones.com

Min Cost= €9, No of Beds = 42, Facilities= KITCHEN, WASHING MACHINE, TUMBLE DRYER, PRIVATE ROOMS AVAILABLE
Opening Times: 11:00 till 23:00 March 1 till November 30
🌐 www.booking.com/hotel/es/albergue-los-blasones.html

Albergue O Durmiñento
- 📍 Rúa Mayor, 44
- 📍 42.77739, -7.41516
- ☎ +34 9 8253 1099
- ☎ +34 6 0086 2508
- ✉ durmiento_sarria@hotmail.com

Min Cost= €10, No of Beds = 41, Facilities= WASHING MACHINE, TUMBLE DRYER, WIFI
Opening Times: 11:00 till 23:00 April 1 till November 30
🌐 www.booking.com/hotel/es/albergue-o-durminento.html

Albergue San Lázaro
- 📍 Calle San Lázaro, 7
- 📍 42.78076, -7.41983
- ☎ +34 9 8253 0626
- ☎ +34 6 5918 5482
- ✉ alberguesanlazaro@hotmail.com
- 🌐 www.alberguesanlazaro.com

Min Cost= €10, No of Beds = 30, Facilities= KITCHEN, WASHING MACHINE, TUMBLE DRYER, WIFI, PRIVATE ROOMS AVAILABLE
Opening Times: 12:00 till 23:00 April 1 till October 31
🏩 www.booking.com/hotel/es/albergue-san-lazaro.html

Albergue Oasis
- Camino de Santiago a Tricastela, 12
- 42.77587, -7.40529
- ☎ +34 9 8253 5516 ☎ +34 6 0594 8644
- ✉ reservas@albergueoasis.com 🏩 www.albergueoasis.com

Min Cost= €12, No of Beds = 27, Facilities= KITCHEN, WIFI
Opening Times: 11:30 till 23:00 March 1 till October 31
🏩 www.booking.com/hotel/es/albergue-oasis.html

Albergue Casa Peltre
- Calle Escalinata Maior, 10   - 42.77687, -7.4133
- ☎ +34 6 0622 6067
- ✉ hola@alberguecasapeltre.es 🏩 alberguecasapeltre.es

Min Cost= €12, No of Beds = 22, Facilities= KITCHEN, WASHING MACHINE, WIFI
Opening Times: 11:00 till 22:30 April 1 till October 31

Albergue Mayor
- Calle Mayor, 64   - 42.77709, -7.41404
- ☎ +34 6 7165 9998
- ✉ alberguemayor@gmail.com 🏩 www.alberguemayor.es

Min Cost= €10, No of Beds = 16, Facilities= KITCHEN, WASHING MACHINE, TUMBLE DRYER, WIFI
Opening Times: 11:00 till 23:00 March 1 till October 31
🏩 www.booking.com/hotel/es/albergue-mayor.html

Albergue Barullo
- Plaza de Galicia 40   - 42.77535, -7.40750
- ☎ +34 6 9810 8755
- ✉ info@alberguebarullo.com 🏩 alberguebarullo.com

Min Cost= €11, No of Beds = 20, Facilities= KITCHEN, WASHING MACHINE, TUMBLE DRYER, WIFI, PRIVATE ROOMS AVAILABLE
Opening Times: 11:00 till 22:00 March 1 till October 31
🏩 www.booking.com/hotel/es/barullo-cafe-bar-albergue-sarria.html

Hostel Andaina
- Rúa Calvo Sotelo, 11   - 42.78343, -7.41779

☏ +34 6 2823 2103
✉ info@hostelandaina.com ⌂ hostelandaina.com
Min Cost= €13, No of Beds = 26, Facilities= KITCHEN, WASHING MACHINE, TUMBLE DRYER, WIFI
Opening Times: 12:00 till 22:00 April thru October
⌂ www.booking.com/hotel/es/andaina.html

Private Rooms Sarria

Hotel Alfonso IX
📍 Rúa do Peregrino, 29 📌 42.77642, -7.41059
☏ +34 9 8253 0005
✉ INFO@ALFONSOIX.COM
⌂ www.alfonsoix.com
👤=80€ 👥=90€

Hotel Roma
📍 Rúa Calvo Sotelo, 2 📌 42.78377, -7.41842
☏ +34 9 8253 2211
⌂ www.hotelroma1930.es
👤=50€ 👥=60€

Hotel Mar de La Plata
📍 Rúa Formigueiros, 5 📌 42.78314, -7.41678
☏ +34 9 8253 0724
✉ reservas@hotelmardeplata.com
⌂ www.hotelmardeplata.com
👤=40€ 👥=58€

DP Cristal
📍 Rúa Calvo Sotelo, 198 📌 42.77564, -7.40634
☏ +34 6 6979 9512
⌂ dpcristal.com
👤=35€ 👥=45€
Amazing breakfast buffet.

Pensión O Camino
📍 Rúa Benigno Quiroga, 16 📌 42.86639, -7.44648
☏ +34 6 2620 5172
✉ pensionocamino@gmail.com
⌂ pensionocaminosarria.com
👤=30€ 👥=40€

La Casona de Sarria

- Rúa San Lázaro, 24
- ☎ +34 9 8253 5556
- ✉ info@lacasonadesarria.es
- 🌐 www.lacasonadesarria.es
- 👤=57€ 👥=57€
- 📍 42.78107, -7.42082
- ☎ +34 6 7003 6444

El Bordón de la Casa Batallón

- Rúa Maior, 29
- ☎ +34 6 2863 6427
- ✉ costalg50@gmail.com
- 🌐 http://casabatallon.com
- 👤=29€ 👥=34€
- 📍 42.77724, -7.41623

Vilei

110.1km to Santiago. 1km to Barbadelo. Altitude 522m. Local Facilities= CAFE/BAR. GPS: 42.76866, -7.44430

Vilei Village Map

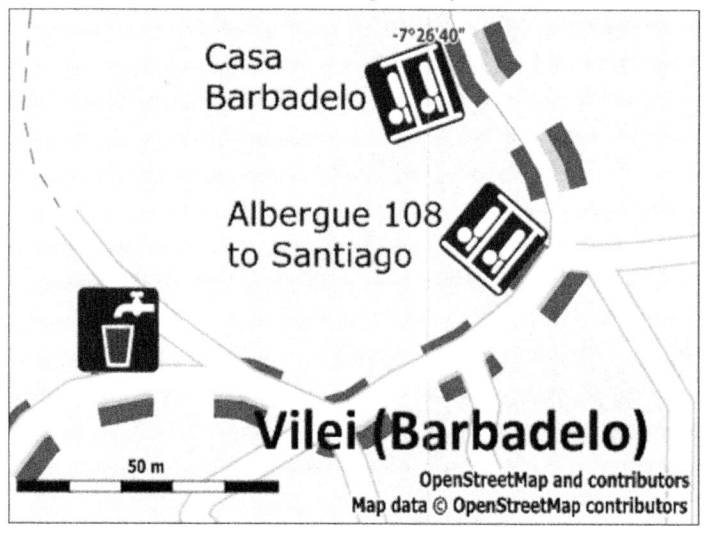

Notes on Vilei

The cafe at the guest house Casa Barbadelo provides a welcome first break of the day and has a nice souvenir shop.

Pilgrim Accommodation Vilei

Albergue Casa Barbadelo
- Vilei
- +34 9 8253 1934
- info@bardelo.com
- 42.76914, -7.44448
- +34 6 5916 0498
- www.barbadelo.com

Min Cost= €10, No of Beds = 70, Facilities= WASHING MACHINE, TUMBLE DRYER, WIFI, SWIMMING POOL, PRIVATE ROOMS AVAILABLE
Opening Times: 12:00 till N/A Holy Week till October 31
www.booking.com/hotel/es/casa-barbadelo.html

Barbadelo

109.1km to Santiago. 0.7km to Rente. Altitude 548m. Local Facilities= CAFE/BAR. GPS: 42.76587, -7.45029

Barbadelo Village Map

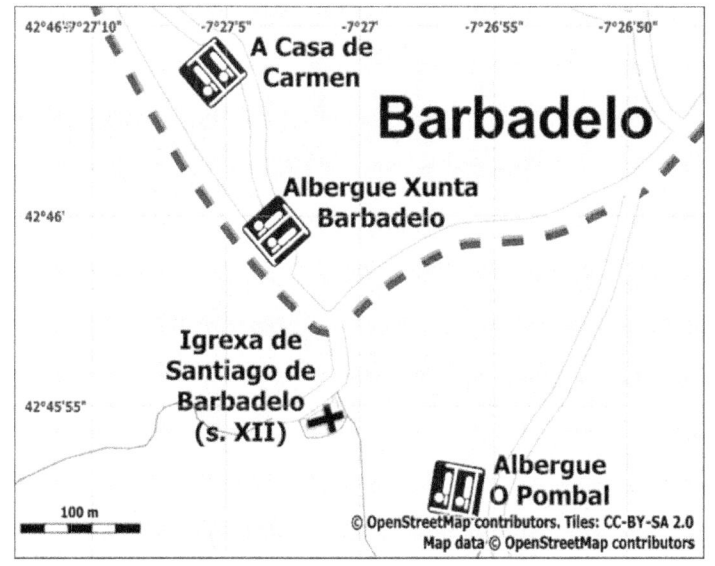

Notes on Barbadelo

Barbadelo is a small village now but was important enough (along with Portomarín, Palas de Rey, Leboreiro, Boente, Castaneda, and Ferreiros) to be mentioned in the Codex Calixtinus (The Codex Calixtinus is a 12th century manuscript which is regarded as the first ever guidebook for the Camino, in fact it is regarded as the first ever guidebook in Europe). At that time, the village had a monastery dependent on the large abbey at Samos. All that remains of its former importance is the 12th century Romanesque church of Santiago de Barbadelo.

Pilgrim Accommodation Barbadelo

Albergue Xunta
- Old school, Vilei
- 42.76623, -7.45081
- ☎ +34 6 8225 2087
- ☎ +34 6 8130 9155

Min Cost= €8, No of Beds = 18, Facilities= WASHING MACHINE, TUMBLE DRYER

Opening Times: 13:00 till 22:00. Open all year.

Albergue O Pombal
- Close to the Church
- 42.76469, -7.44889
- ☎ +34 6 8671 8732
- albergueopombal@gmail.com
- www.albergueopombal.blogspot.co.uk

Min Cost= €10, No of Beds = 8, Facilities= KITCHEN, WASHING MACHINE, TUMBLE DRYER

Opening Times: 13:00 till 23:00 Holy Week till October 31

Casa Albergue Molino de Marzán
- km 104.5, Marzán (Barbadelo)
- 42.7723, -7.48155
- ☎ +34 6 7943 8077
- adm@molinomarzan.com
- www.molinomarzan.com

Min Cost= €10, No of Beds = 16, Facilities= KITCHEN, WASHING MACHINE, TUMBLE DRYER, WIFI

Opening Times: 12:00 till 22:00 March 1 till October 31

Rente

108.5km to Santiago. 0.7km to A Serra. Altitude 594m. Local Facilities= HOTEL OR GUEST HOUSE TYPE ACCOMMODATION. GPS: 42.76810, -7.45900

Private Rooms Rente

Casa Nova de Rente
- 42.76870, -7.46013
- +34 9 8218 7854
- casaruralnovaderente@hotmail.com
- www.casanovaderente.com
- ♦=34€ ♦♦=34€

A Serra

107.8km to Santiago. 3.1km to Peruscallo. Altitude 630m. Local Facilities= CAFE/BAR, RESTAURANT. GPS: 42.77099, -7.46704

Peruscallo

104.6km to Santiago. 2.8km to Morgade. Altitude 633m. Local Facilities= CAFE/BAR. GPS: 42.78059, -7.49346

Notes on Peruscallo

Just before Persucallo there is a small bakery which doubles as a café. At peak season it is often overwhelmed and the queues for the toilets are often long.

Morgade

101.9km to Santiago. 1.4km to Ferreiros. Altitude 651m. Local Facilities= CAFE/BAR, RESTAURANT. GPS: 42.78215, -7.52122

Notes on Morgade

The first bar in Morgade is new and often overcrowded. Personally, I find that the second bar, Casa Morgade, provides a better option with it's made to order omelettes which are excellent. At either bar the toilets provide a truly welcome comfort break especially for female pilgrims.

Pilgrim Accommodation Morgade

Albergue Casa Morgade
- Km 101.996
- +34 6 7653 5369
- 42.75212, -7.52122
- casamorgade.gal/en

Min Cost= €10, No of Beds = 16, Facilities= WASHING MACHINE, TUMBLE DRYER, PRIVATE ROOMS AVAILABLE
Opening Times: 12:00 till 23:00 Holy Week till October 31

Ferreiros

100.5km to Santiago. 0.3km to Mirallos. Altitude 660m. Local Facilities= RESTAURANT. GPS: 42.78316, -7.53276

Ferreiros Village Map

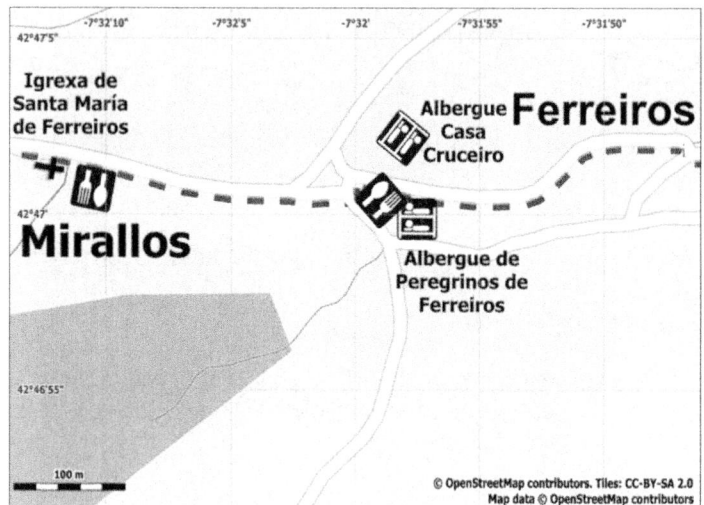

Notes on Ferreiros

Ferreiros translates as blacksmiths as this was originally the location where pilgrims on horseback could get the blacksmith to re-shoe their horses.

As Ferreiros is about 700 metres from the 100km marker, some pilgrims (especially those on escorted tours) will start their pilgrimage from here rather than Sarria.

Both Casa Cruceiros and O Mirallos are good alternative lunch breaks. Perhaps not quite to the standard of Casa Morgade but none the less particularly good places for a lunch break.

Pilgrim Accommodation Ferreiros

Albergue Xunta
- Ferreiros
- ☎ +34 6 9996 8886

- 42.78318, -7.53283
- ☎ +34 6 3896 2809

Min Cost= €8, No of Beds = 22, Facilities= WASHING MACHINE, TUMBLE DRYER.
Opening Times: 13:00 till 22:00. Open all year.

Albergue Casa Cruceiro
- km 100.746
- +34 9 8254 1240
- casacruceirodeferreiros@gmail.com
- www.casacruceirodeferreiros.com

- 42.784, -7.53289
- +34 6 3902 0064

Min Cost= €10, No of Beds = 12, Facilities= WASHING MACHINE, TUMBLE DRYER, PRIVATE ROOMS AVAILABLE
Opening Times: 11:30 till 00:00 March 1 till November 30

Mirallos

100.2km to Santiago. 0.5km to A Pena. Altitude 638m. Local Facilities= NONE. GPS: 42.78380, -7.53652

Notes on Mirallos

Mirallos houses the small but elegant 12th century Romanesque church of Santa María de Ferreiros. Originally situated in Ferreiros it was moved stone by stone to its current location in 1790 following a change in the path of the Camino. Like many churches on the Camino it has a beautifully kept walled cemetery attached.

A Pena

99.7km to Santiago. 0.7km to As Rozas. Altitude 644m. Local Facilities= HOTEL OR GUEST HOUSE TYPE ACCOMMODATION. GPS: 42.78541, -7.54263

As Rozas

98.9km to Santiago. 1.8km to Mercadoiro. Altitude 639m. Local Facilities= CAFE/BAR. GPS: 42.78402, -7.54974

Notes on As Rozas

As Rozas contains a beautiful donativo oasis called Hospitalidad al peregrino which is well worth a visit.

Mercadoiro

97.1km to Santiago. 1.7km to A Parrocha. Altitude 547m. Local Facilities= CAFE/BAR, RESTAURANT. GPS: 42.78873, -7.56866

Notes on Mercadoiro

The courtyard of Albergue Mercadoiro houses a café / bar which makes one of my favourite afternoon stops.

Pilgrim Accommodation Mercadoiro

Albergue Mercadoiro
- Aldea de Mercadoiro, 2 (km 95.3)
- 42.78522, -7.56884   ☎ +34 9 8254 5359
- canillasfuentes@hotmail.com
- www.mercadoiro.com

Min Cost= €12, No of Beds = 34, Facilities= WASHING MACHINE, TUMBLE DRYER, WIFI, PRIVATE ROOMS AVAILABLE

Opening Times: No check-in restrictions. March 1 till November 15

www.booking.com/hotel/es/mercadoiro.es.html
Currently up for sale

A Parrocha

95.4km to Santiago. 1.3km to Vilachá. Altitude 489m. Local Facilities= CAFÉ/BAR, RESTAURANTE. GPS : 42.79401, -7.58755

Vilachá

94.0km to Santiago. 1.8km to Portomarín. Altitude 424m. Local Facilities= RESTAURANT, CAFÉ/BAR. GPS: 42.79561, -7.60353

Notes on Vilachá

Vilachá hosts two good albergues and a vegetarian restaurant which doubles as an excellent bar and pleasant last stop before Portomarín. As Portomarín is often a pinch point for overnight accommodation, Vilachá offers a nice off-stage alternative especially if you are planning a six-day Camino.

Pilgrim Accommodation Vilachá

Albergue Vilachá
- Calle Camino de Santiago, Vilachá
- 42.79539, -7.60387   ☎ +34 6 9600 4491
- alberguevilacha@gmail.com
- www.facebook.com/Albergue-Bar-Vilach%C3%A1-100606848397125

Min Cost= €14, No of Beds = 10, Facilities = WASHING MACHINE, TUMBLE DRYER, WIFI
Opening Times: 12:00 till 22:00 April 1 till October 31
👑 www.booking.com/hotel/es/albergue-vilacha.es.html

Albergue Casa Banderas
- Calle Camino de Santiago, Vilachá, 5
- 42.79554, -7.60301   ☎ +34 6 8217 9589
- 👑 www.casabanderas.com

Min Cost= €14, No of Beds = 11, Facilities = WASHING MACHINE, TUMBLE DRYER, COMMUNAL MEAL, WIFI
Opening Times: 12:00 till 22:00 April 1 till October 31
WhatsApp is the preferred method of communication. Run by a very kind Californian couple Ray and Dominique.

Portomarín

92.2km to Santiago. 7.7km to Gonzar. Altitude 388m. Local Facilities= CAFE/BAR, RESTAURANT, ATM, HOTEL OR GUEST HOUSE TYPE ACCOMMODATION, PHARMACY, MEDICAL CENTRE, GROCERY STORE. GPS: 42.80768, -7.61570

Notes on Portomarín

If water levels are low, you can see parts of the submerged old town on your left as you cross the long bridge into Portomarín. The current bridge is from the 1960s but there has been a bridge here since Roman times.

The creation in 1963 of the reservoir of Belesar, on the river Miño, flooded the old village of Portomarín. Its main historic buildings were rescued and moved stone by stone to the new relocated village still known as Portomarín. These included the 10th century Romanesque church of San Pedro and the 12th century fortress church of San Nicolás which is now in the main square and it is here that most evenings the Pilgrim Mass is said. If you look carefully on parts of both the inside and outside of the church, you can still see the numbering of the stones which was used to ensure the correct reconstruction of the church.

Although this is one of the few wine growing regions on this part of the Camino, Portomarín is more famous for its Aguardente liquor called Orujo which is normally drunk as a digestive and for which Portomarín hosts an annual fiesta on Easter Sunday.

Because there are no villages with albergues within easy distance beyond Portomarín, Portomarín is often fully booked. It is best to avoid this situation by booking at least a few days in advance. However, if you do find yourself in this difficult situation, the town hall, which is in the main square, will open a sports hall or primary school and allow you to sleep on the floor overnight.

When leaving Portomarín in the morning there are very few cafe/bars open for breakfast. However, it is worth taking breakfast here since the next rest stop with a cafe/bar is over 8km away.

The first kilometre or two of today's hike out of Portomarín is well shaded but it is the steepest part of today's climb. Fortunately, the steepness eases off as you exit the woods.

Portomarín Village Map

A Albergue Folgueira
B Albergue Aqua
C Pensión Casa Pérez
D Albergue Ferramenteiro
E Albergue Pons Minea
F Casona da Ponte
G Albergue Casa Cruz
H Albergue Novo Porto
I Albergue El Caminante
J Albergue Ultreia
K Albergue Porto Santiago
L Albergue Pasiño a Pasino

M Youth Hostel
N Albergue Villamartín
O Casa do Maestro
P Municipal Albergue
Q Albergue Manuel
R Hostal El Padrino
S Hotel Pazo de Berbetoros
T Pensión Portomiño
U Albergue Casa do Marabillas
V Pousada De Portomarin
W Capela das Neves
X Iglesia de San Nicolás
Y Iglesia de San Pedro

Pilgrim Accommodation Portomarín

Albergue Xunta
- Rúa Fraga Iribarne
- ☏ +34 6 3896 2810

- 42.80843, -7.61496
- ☏ +34 6 6039 6816

Min Cost= €8, No of Beds = 80, Facilities= KITCHEN, WASHING MACHINE, TUMBLE DRYER
Opening Times: 13:00 till 22:00. Open all year.

Albergue Ferramentiero
- Calle Chantada, 3
- 42.8062, -7.6182
- +34 9 8254 5362
- info@albergueferramenteiro.com
- www.albergueferramenteiro.com

Min Cost= €12, No of Beds = 130, Facilities= KITCHEN, WASHING MACHINE, TUMBLE DRYER, WIFI
Opening Times: 12:00 till 23:00 Holy Week till October 31
- www.booking.com/hotel/es/albergue-ferramenteiro.html

Albergue Folgueira
- Avenida de Chantada, 18
- 42.8066, -7.61975
- +34 9 8254 5166
- +34 6 5944 5651
- info@alberguefolgueira.com
- alberguefolgueira.com

Min Cost= €12, No of Beds = 32, Facilities= KITCHEN, WASHING MACHINE, TUMBLE DRYER, WIFI
Opening Times: 10:00 till 23:00. Open all year.
- www.booking.com/hotel/es/albergue-folgueira.html

Albergue Pasiño a Pasiño
- Rúa de Compostela, 25
- 42.80685, -7.61654
- +34 6 6566 7243
- alberguepasoapaso@gmail.com
- pasinapasin.es

Min Cost= €12, No of Beds = 30, Facilities= KITCHEN, WASHING MACHINE, TUMBLE DRYER, WIFI
Opening Times: 12:00 till 23:00. Open all year.

Albergue Novo Porto
- Calle Benigno Quiroga, 12
- 42.80722, -7.61688
- +34 6 1043 6736
- info@alberguenovoporto.com
- alberguenovoporto.com

Min Cost= €12, No of Beds = 22, Facilities= KITCHEN, WASHING MACHINE, TUMBLE DRYER, WIFI
Opening Times: 10:00 till 23:30 April 1 till November 30

Albergue Villamartin
- Rúa dos Peregrino, 1
- 42.80716, -7.61492

☏ +34 9 8254 5054
✉ reservas@hotelvillajardin.com
🌐 alberguevillamartin.webnode.es
Min Cost= €10, No of Beds = 22, Facilities = KITCHEN, WASHING MACHINE, TUMBLE DRYER, WIFI
Opening Times: 12:00 till 23:00 April 1 till October 31

Albergue Casa Cruz
📍 Calle Benigno Quiroga, 16   📍 42.80714, -7.61698
☏ +34 9 8254 5140   ☏ +34 6 5220 4548
✉ info@casacruzportomarin.com
🌐 www.casacruzportomarin.com
Min Cost= €10, No of Beds = 16, Facilities= WASHING MACHINE, TUMBLE DRYER, WIFI
Opening Times: Closes at 23:00. Open all year.

Albergue Manuel
📍 Rúa do Miño, 1   📍 42.80866, -7.61437
☏ +34 9 8254 5385   ☏ +34 6 7975 4718
✉ pensionmanuel1@gmail.com   🌐 www.pensionmanuel.es
Min Cost= €10, No of Beds = 16, Facilities= KITCHEN, WASHING MACHINE, TUMBLE DRYER, WIFI
Opening Times: 12:00. April 1 till November 30

Albergue Porto Santiago
📍 Calle Diputación, 8   📍 42.80807, -7.61678
☏ +34 6 1882 6515
✉ info@albergueportosantiago.com
🌐 www.albergueportosantiago.com
Min Cost= €12, No of Beds = 16, Facilities= KITCHEN, WASHING MACHINE, TUMBLE DRYER, WIFI
Opening Times: 12:00 till 23:00. Open all year.

Albergue Ultreia
📍 Calle Diputación, 9   📍 42.80796, -7.61672
☏ +34 9 8254 5067   ☏ +34 6 7660 7292
✉ info@ultreiaportomarin.com   🌐 www.ultreiaportomarin.com
Min Cost= €12, No of Beds = 14, Facilities= KITCHEN, WASHING MACHINE, TUMBLE DRYER, WIFI
Opening Times: 11:00 till 23:00. Open all year.

Albergue El Caminante
📍 Calle Sánchez Carro, 7   📍 42.80744, -7.61658

☎ +34 9 8254 5176
✉ info@pensionelcaminante.com 🕸 pensionelcaminante.com
Min Cost= €10, No of Beds = 12, Facilities= WASHING MACHINE, TUMBLE DRYER, WIFI, PRIVATE ROOMS AVAILABLE
Opening Times: 12:00 till 00:00 Holy Week till October 31

Albergue Aqua
📍 Calle Barreiros, 2   📍 42.80745, -7.61824
☎ +34 6 0892 1372
✉ albergueaquaportomarin@hotmail.com
Min Cost= €12, No of Beds = 10, Facilities= KITCHEN, WASHING MACHINE, TUMBLE DRYER, WIFI, PRIVATE ROOMS AVAILABLE
Opening Times: 13:00 till 22:00 March 1 till October 31
🕸 www.booking.com/hotel/es/albergue-aqua-portomarin.html

Albergue Casona da Ponte
📍 Camiño da Capela, 10   📍 42.80573, -7.61764
☎ +34 6 8611 2877   ☎ +34 9 8216 9862
✉ casonadaponte@gmail.com   🕸 casonadaponte.com
Min Cost= €10, No of Beds = 47, Facilities= KITCHEN, WASHING MACHINE, TUMBLE DRYER, WIFI
Opening Times: 11:30 till 23:00 March 1 till October 31

Casa Marabillas
📍 Camiño do Monte, 3   📍 42.81009, -7.61586
☎ +34 7 4445 0425   ☎ +34 9 8218 9086
✉ casadomarabillas@gmail.com
🕸 www.casadomarabillas.com
Min Cost= €15, No of Beds = 10, Facilities= KITCHEN, WASHING MACHINE, TUMBLE DRYER, WIFI, PRIVATE ROOMS AVAILABLE
Opening Times: No check-in restrictions. Open all year.

Albergue Pons Minea
📍 Avenida de Sarria, 11   📍 42.80591, -7.61707
☎ +34 9 8254 5364   ☎ +34 6 8645 6931
✉ info@ponsminea.es   🕸 ponsminea.es
Min Cost= €12, No of Beds = 24, Facilities= KITCHEN, WASHING MACHINE, TUMBLE DRYER, WIFI, PRIVATE ROOMS AVAILABLE
Opening Times: 12:00 till 19:30. Open all year.
🕸 www.booking.com/hotel/es/pons-minea.html

Albergue Huellas
📍 Rúa do Peregrino, 15   📍 42.80672, -7.61550

☏ +34 6 8139 8278   ☏ +34 9 8254 5340
✉ info.alberguehuellas@gmail.com
🕸 www.alberguehuellas.com
Min Cost= €16, No of Beds = 6, Facilities= KITCHEN, WASHING MACHINE, TUMBLE DRYER, WIFI, PRIVATE ROOMS AVAILABLE
Opening Times: 11:00. Open all year.
🕸 www.booking.com/hotel/es/huellas-albergue-turistico.html

Private Rooms Portomarín

Spa Hotel Vistalegre
📍 Calle Compostela, 29   📍 42.80627, -7.61676
☏ +34 9 8254 5076
✉ info@vistalegrehotel.com
🕸 www.vistalegrehotel.com
👤=80€ 👥=80€

Pousada de Portomarin
📍 Rúa do Parador   📍 42.80975, -7.61463
☏ +34 9 8254 5200
✉ info@pousadadeportomarin.es
🕸 www.pousadadeportomarin.es
👤=60€ 👥=75€
Outdoor swimming pool.

Hostal El Padrino
📍 Rúa Fraga Iribarne, 18   📍 42.80888, -7.61477
☏ +34 6 6558 6070
✉ hostalelpadrino@gmail.com
🕸 hostalelpadrino.com
👤=60€ 👥=70€
Godfather themed hotel with a nice Jacuzzi.

Casa do Maestro
📍 Rúa Fraga Iribarne, 1   📍 42.80796, -7.61516
☏ +34 6 2651 0806   ☏ +34 9 8254 5318
✉ info@casadomaestro.com
🕸 casadomaestro.com
👤=50€ 👥=70€

Hotel VillaJardín
📍 Rúa do Miño, 14   📍 42.80744, -7.61511
☏ +34 9 8254 5054
✉ reservas@hotelvillajardin.com

🕸 hotelvillajardin.com
👤=45€ 👤👤=60€

Pensión Mar
📍 Rúa Fraga Iribarne, 5
☎ +34 6 2261 1211
✉ info@pensionmar.com
🕸 www.pensionmar.com
👤=35€ 👤👤=48€

📍 42.80813, -7.61495
☎ +34 6 3038 9641

A Fontana De Luxo
📍 Fontedagra, 2
☎ +34 6 4564 9496
✉ info@afontanadeluxo.com
🕸 afontanadeluxo.com
👤=28€ 👤👤=96€

📍 42.80107, -7.61709

The entrance arch (below) is made from one of the arches of the original bridge and is one of my favourite sites as it gives you the feeling of arriving.

Chapter 5 - Portomarín to Palas de Rei

From	Waypoint	Decimal GPS	Distance	3.9 km/hr	4.6 km/hr	5.3 km/hr
Portomarín	Gonzar	42.82651 -7.69629	7.7km	2hrs 30mins	2hrs 7mins	1hrs 50mins
Gonzar	Castromaior	42.83173 -7.70877	1.1km	0hrs 22mins	0hrs 19mins	0hrs 16mins
Castromaior	Hospital da Cruz	42.84081 -7.73411	2.5km	0hrs 48mins	0hrs 41mins	0hrs 35mins
Hospital da Cruz	Ventas de Narón	42.84412 -7.74881	1.5km	0hrs 27mins	0hrs 23mins	0hrs 20mins
Ventas de Narón	Alto de Ligonde	42.84847 -7.75871	0.9km	0hrs 17mins	0hrs 14mins	0hrs 12mins
Alto de Ligonde	Ligonde	42.85897 -7.77990	2.0km	0hrs 33mins	0hrs 28mins	0hrs 24mins
Ligonde	Airexe	42.86531 -7.78714	0.9km	0hrs 16mins	0hrs 13mins	0hrs 12mins
Airexe	Portos	42.87355 -7.80710	1.8km	0hrs 33mins	0hrs 28mins	0hrs 24mins
Portos	Lestedo	42.87218 -7.81411	0.7km	0hrs 14mins	0hrs 12mins	0hrs 10mins
Lestedo	Os Valos	42.87317 -7.82173	0.7km	0hrs 14mins	0hrs 12mins	0hrs 10mins
Os Valos	A Brea	42.87586 -7.83606	1.2km	0hrs 21mins	0hrs 18mins	0hrs 16mins
A Brea	Os Chacotes	42.87392 -7.85711	1.9km	0hrs 33mins	0hrs 28mins	0hrs 24mins
Os Chacotes	Palas de Rei	42.87278 -7.86843	1.0km	0hrs 16mins	0hrs 14mins	0hrs 12mins
Portomarín	Palas de Rei	42.87278 -7.86843	24.1km	7hrs 31mins	6hrs 22mins	5hrs 32mins

Portomarín to Palas de Rei Elevation Chart

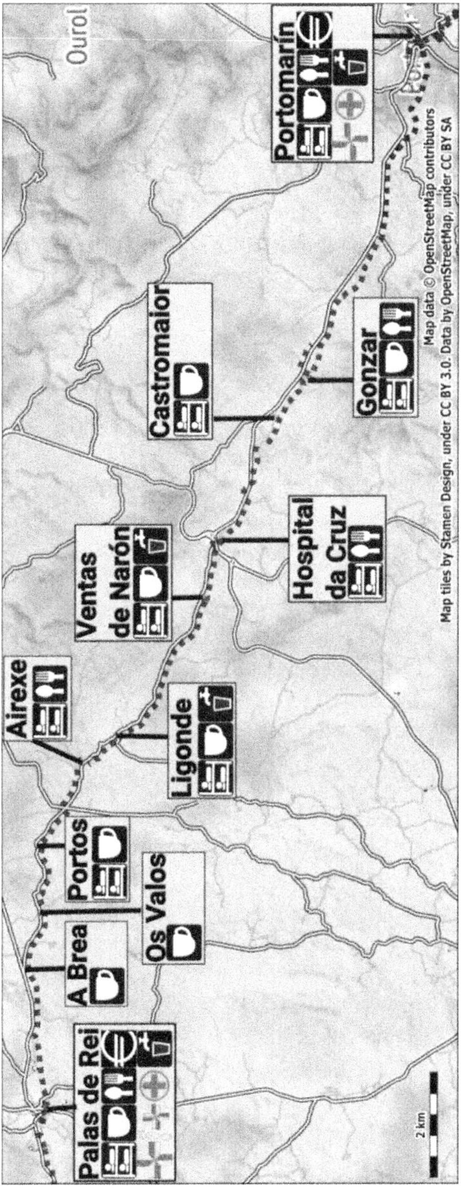
Ourol
Portomarín
Castromaior
Gonzar
Hospital da Cruz
Ventas de Narón
Ligonde
Airexe
Portos
Os Valos
A Brea
Palas de Rei
2 km
Map data © OpenStreetMap contributors
Map tiles by Stamen Design, under CC BY 3.0. Data by OpenStreetMap, under CC BY SA

Notes about Today's Stage

Your second day starts with a short but steep descent to rejoin the Camino at the entrance of Portomarín. You then cross another part of the dam. After you cross the dam, you will be presented with the choice of turning left and following the measured route along the road or turning right on the complementary route. My strong preference is to take the complementary route through the trees. Today's ascent is about 450 metres over 9 km which is moderately demanding but is generally well shaded. The first opportunity for a break comes at about the 8km mark and three quarters up the climb in Gonzar. The next opportunity for a break comes another 1 or 2km further in Castromaior. Another 3km further is Hospital da Cruz and by this point although there is a small amount of moderate climbing left, you have completed the main ascent and it is here or in Ventas de Narón that most people choose to have their lunch break. Shortly after Hospital da Cruz you will pass through Ventas de Narón just before reaching the peak of today's walk at Alto de Ligonde (724 metres). After Alto de Ligonde, the countryside is best described as rolling, descending through Ligonde and your last opportunity for a break today in Lestedo. Although 4km longer than yesterday and with a big climb today does not have the sharp descents which slowed you down yesterday. In total today's walk should take you about 7 and a half hours plus breaks.

Gonzar

84.5km to Santiago. 1.1km to Castromayor. Altitude 551m. Local Facilities= CAFE/BAR. GPS: 42.82647, -7.69639

Gonzar Village Map

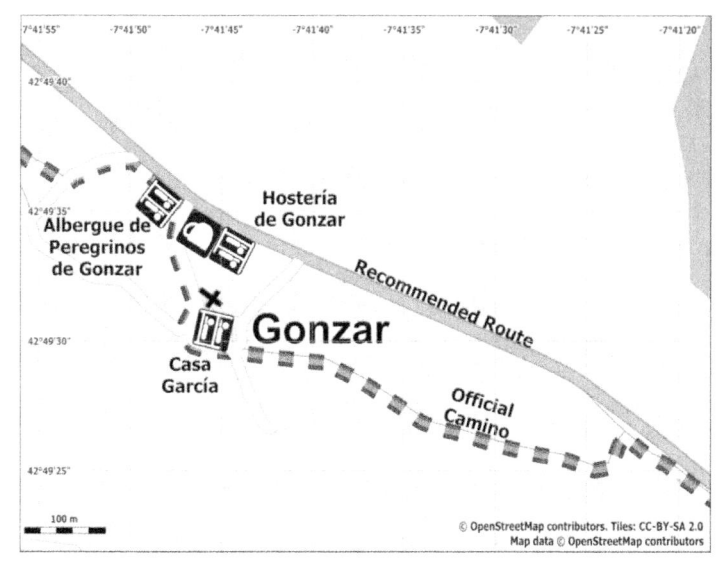

Pilgrim Accommodation Gonzar

Albergue Xunta
- Beside the road
- +34 6 6039 6817
- 42.82639, -7.69613
- +34 6 3896 2811

Min Cost= €8, No of Beds = 30, Facilities= WASHING MACHINE, TUMBLE DRYER

Opening Times: 13:00 till 22:00. Open all year.

Albergue Casa Garcia
- Gonzar, 8
- +34 9 8215 7842
- 42.82515, -7.69621

www.facebook.com/Casa-Garcia-102482276760927

Min Cost= €10, No of Beds = 26, Facilities= WASHING MACHINE, TUMBLE DRYER, PRIVATE ROOMS AVAILABLE

Opening Times: 12:00 till 23:00 Holy Week till November 30

Hostería de Gonzar
- Lugar de Gonzar, 7
- +34 9 8215 4878
- info@hosteriadegonzar.com
- 42.82546, -7.69322
- +34 6 8960 9407
- hosteriadegonzar.com

Min Cost= €12, No of Beds = 16, Facilities= WIFI, WASHING MACHINE, TUMBLE DRYER, SWIMMING POOL, PRIVATE ROOMS AVAILABLE
Opening Times: 12:00 till 22:00 Holy Week till October 31
🕸 www.booking.com/hotel/es/hosteria-de-gonzar.html

Notes on Gonzar

The hike up to Gonzar is a long and demanding hike mostly through woods but with big chunks by the roadside. Just before you reach Gonzar you have the choice of following the Camino through the village or staying on the main road. Whilst I would normally advocate the few hundred extra metres for a gentle stroll through the village, at this point I think most people need a break and I would advise going with the road route up to the cafe which is nearby. The cafe on the roadside next door to the albergue does very good hot plates (my favourite being the amazing eggs and French fries) of food but is often very busy. If it is too busy, Albergue Ortiz is less than a kilometre away and has a café. Additionally, there is another small cafe in Castromaior just over a kilometre away which is my personal favourite if the bar in Gonzar is overwhelmed.

Castromaior

83.3km to Santiago. 2.5km to Hospital da Cruz. Altitude 601m. Local Facilities= CAFE/BAR, HOTEL OR GUEST HOUSE TYPE ACCOMMODATION. GPS: 42.83174, -7.7087

Pilgrim Accommodation Castromaior

Albergue Ortiz
- Castromaior, 2
- 42.83058, -7.70432
- ☏ +34 9 8209 9416
- ✉ info@albergueortiz.com
- 🕸 albergueortiz.com

Min Cost= €10, No of Beds = 18, Facilities= WASHING MACHINE, TUMBLE DRYER, WIFI
Opening Times: 10:00 till 22:30 March 1 till November 30

Private Rooms Castromaior

Casa Perdigueira

📞 42.83176, -7.70915
☎ +34 6 9085 2026
👤=36€ 👥=36€

Notes on Castromaior

Castromaior gets its name from the original Celtic hill fort (castro) and there has been an archaeological excavation of this original iron age settlement (which dates from the second century BC to the first century AD). This archaeological excavation is in the area to your left just after you leave Castromaior itself. The local authorities are not keen to promote the site in case an influx of visitors damages the site. What is also worth visiting in Castromaior is the small but well-preserved 12th century Romanesque church of Santa María de Castromaior which has a wooden Romanesque statue of the Virgin as well as a Baroque retablo.

Hospital da Cruz

80.8km to Santiago. 1.5km to Ventas de Narón. Altitude 679m. Local Facilities= RESTAURANT. GPS: 42.840777, -7.73409

Notes on Hospital da Cruz

The new modern bar at the crossing over the highway is very pleasant but it is somewhat expensive.

Hospital da Cruz Village Map

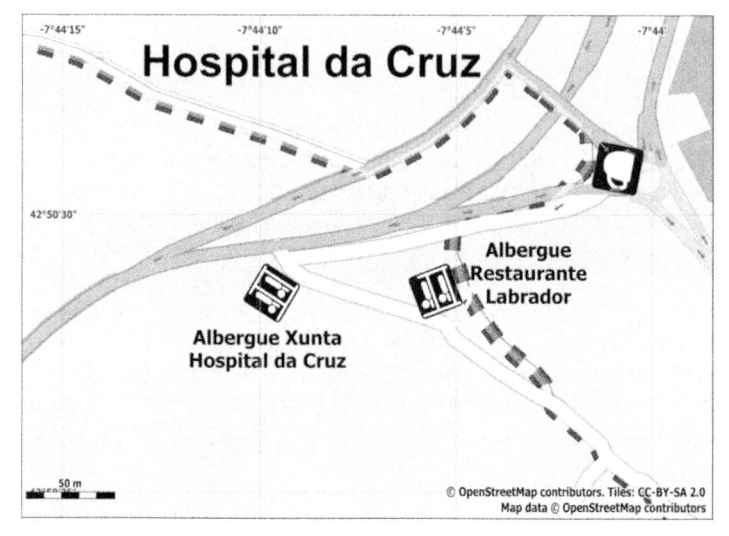

Pilgrim Accommodation Hospital da Cruz

Albergue Xunta
- O Hospital, s/n San Mamede do Río
- 42.84134, -7.73597 ☏ +34 6 6039 6818

Min Cost= €8, No of Beds = 32, Facilities= KITCHEN, WASHING MACHINE, TUMBLE DRYER
Opening Times: 13:00 till 22:00. Open all year.

Ventas de Narón

79.3km to Santiago. 3.0km to Ligonde. Altitude 702m. Local Facilities= CAFE/BAR. GPS: 42.84425, -7.74888

Notes on Ventas de Narón

In medieval times, the town was known as Sala Regine and is mentioned in the Codex Calixtinus. Its current name Ventas (meaning sales) possibly indicates that it was once a place of trade on the Camino. It had a pilgrim hostel built in the 13th century by the Knights Templar of which the only remaining part is the Capilla de Santa María Magdalena on the outskirts of the hamlet. If you wish to access to this chapel, there is a phone number on the door you can ring and somebody from the village will come and open it for you. The village was also the site of a battle in 820 to defeat the invading forces of the Emir of Córdoba. Now it is nothing more than a peaceful hamlet that provides an excellent opportunity for lunch. Both café bars in Ventas have good food but my preference is for Casa Molar.

Ventas de Narón Village Map

Pilgrim Accommodation Ventas de Narón

Albergue Casa Molar
- Ventas de Narón, 4
- 42.84422, -7.74776
- +34 6 9679 4507
- casamolar_ventas@yahoo.es
- casamolar-hostel.negocio.site

Min Cost= €12, No of Beds = 18, Facilities= WASHING MACHINE, TUMBLE DRYER, WIFI, PRIVATE ROOMS AVAILABLE
Opening Times: 11:00 till 23:00 March 1 till November 30

Albergue O Cruceiro
- Ventas de Narón, 6
- 42.84398, -7.74921
- +34 6 5806 4917
- albergueocruceiro@gmail.com
- www.albergueocruceiro.blogspot.com

Min Cost= €10, No of Beds = 22, Facilities= WASHING MACHINE, TUMBLE DRYER, WIFI, PRIVATE ROOMS AVAILABLE

Opening Times: 12:00 till 23:00 March 1 till December 31

Ligonde

76.4km to Santiago. 0.9km to Airexe. Altitude 628m. Local Facilities= CAFE/BAR. GPS: 42.85890, -7.77987

Notes on Ligonde

About 300 metres (42.85523, -7.77739) before you reach Ligonde you come across the Cruceiro de Ligonde (the stone cross of Ligonde). This dates from 1670 and is one of the best known Cruceiros on the whole Camino Francés. On one side can be seen the image of the Virgin with Christ in her arms and on the other side you can see Christ on the cross and at the foot of Christ a skull.

Ligonde was the home of a pilgrim hospital from 956 till 1753 together with a pilgrim cemetery. All that remains today of the cemetery is a simple cross on a stone wall.

The Albergue Fuente del Peregrino in Ligonde offers donativo tea, coffee, water and fruit. On a hot day this is welcome refreshment, but I normally prefer to take an extended break at Casa Mariluz which is about another 500m further.

Just after Ligonde by the municipal albergue the Camino cuts off the corner, but the path can be quite tricky. If you do not have walking poles, I would recommend walking the extra few metres and stay on the road.

Ligonde Village Map

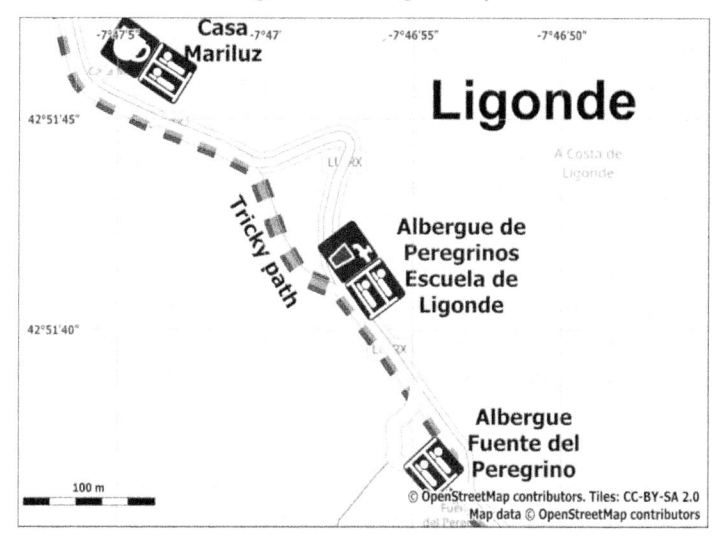

Pilgrim Accommodation Ligonde

Albergue Fuente del Peregrino
- Ligonde, 4
- 42.86011, -7.78153
- +34 6 8755 0527
- lafuentedelperegrino@agape.org
- lafuentedelperegrino.com/en

Min Cost= €Don., No of Beds = 7, Facilities= COMMUNAL MEAL
Opening Times: 13:00 till 22:00 April 1 till October 31

Airexe/Eirexe

75.5km to Santiago. 1.8km to Portos. Altitude 632m. Local Facilities= RESTAURANT, HOTEL OR GUEST HOUSE TYPE ACCOMMODATION. GPS: 42.86541, -7.78727

Notes on Airexe/Eirexe

To clear the confusion, Airexe is the Galician name for this village and Eirexe is the Castilian (Spanish) name for this village. Of note is the small 13th century Iglesia de Santiago.

Airexe/Eirexe Village Map

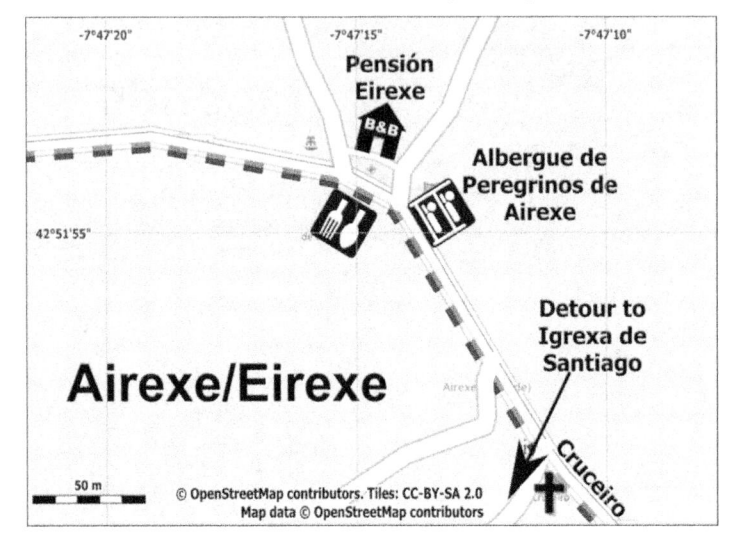

Pilgrim Accommodation Airexe/Eirexe

Pensión Eirexe
- 42.86574, -7.78719
- +34 9 8215 3475
- +34 6 5096 5873
- pensioneirexe@yahoo.es
- www.facebook.com/pages/Pension-Eirexe/321016547997121

Min Cost= €20, No of Beds = 4, Facilities= PRIVATE ROOMS AVAILABLE
Opening Times: 12:00 till 23:00. Open all year.

Albergue Xunta
- Airexe, s/n Monterroso
- 42.86542, -7.78708
- +34 9 8215 3483
- +34 6 6039 6819

Min Cost= €8, No of Beds = 20, Facilities= KITCHEN, WASHING MACHINE, TUMBLE DRYER
Opening Times: 13:00 till 22:00. Open all year.

Portos

73.6km to Santiago. 0.7km to Lestedo. Altitude 583m. Local Facilities= RESTAURANT. GPS: 42.87355, -7.80706

Notes on Portos/Lestedo

The enormous ant statues in O Paso da Formiga (which translates as the passage of the ants) are strange but amazing and the Spanish omelette is pretty good too! Portos makes for a good afternoon stop.

Portos/Lestedo Village Map

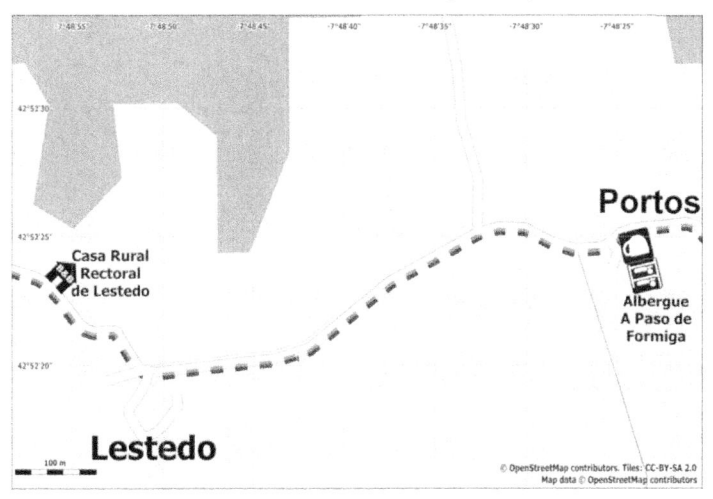

Pilgrim Accommodation Portos

Albergue A Paso do Formiga
- Portos nº4. Lestedo
- 42.87349, -7.80706
- +34 6 1898 4605
- apasodeformiga@hotmail.com
- apasodeformiga.com

Min Cost= €12, No of Beds = 12, Facilities= WASHING MACHINE, TUMBLE DRYER, WIFI, PRIVATE ROOMS AVAILABLE
Opening Times: 10:00 till 22:00 Holy Week till October 31

Lestedo

73.0km to Santiago. 0.7km to Os Valos. Altitude 599m. Local Facilities= HOTEL OR GUEST HOUSE TYPE ACCOMMODATION. GPS: 42.87218, -7.81418

Private Rooms Lestedo

Casa Rectoral de Lestedo
- 42.87290, -7.81534
- ☏ +34 9 8219 6563   ☏ +34 6 6599 4366
- ✉ reservas@rectoraldelestedo.com
- 🏠 rectoraldelestedo.com
- ♂=85€ ♂♂=90€

Very nice bar, open for passing pilgrims.

Os Valos

72.2km to Santiago. 1.2km to A Brea. Altitude 630m. Local Facilities= CAFE/BAR, HOTEL OR GUEST HOUSE TYPE ACCOMMODATION. GPS: 42.87317, -7.821731

Private Rooms Os Valos

Hostería Calixtino
- 42.87248, -7.82180
- ☏ +34 6 7050 0900
- 🏠 hosteriacalixtino.com
- ♂=57€ ♂♂=72€

Nice bar about 30m from the Camino.

A Brea

71.0km to Santiago. 1.9km to Os Chacotes. Altitude 621m. Local Facilities= CAFE/BAR, RESTAURANT. GPS: 42.87589, -7.83604

Os Chacotes

69.1km to Santiago. 1km to Palas de Rei. Altitude 609m. Local Facilities= CAFE/BAR, RESTAURANT, MEDICAL CENTRE. GPS: 42.87392, -7.85711

Notes on Os Chacotes

If you prefer staying in the countryside rather than the town then this may be for you. However, its modern but basic style is not for me. For me Os Chacotes has the feel of a sports resort rather than a pilgrim's hostel and it is 1km to the nearest shops or restaurants in Palas de Rei itself.

Os Chacotes Village Map

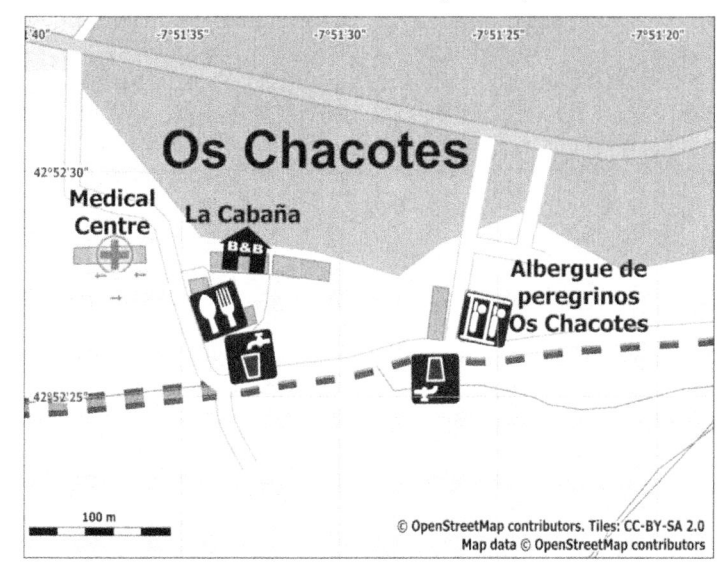

Pilgrim Accommodation Os Chacotes

Albergue Xunta
- Lugar de Chacotes, s/n
- 42.87408, -7.85718
- +34 6 0748 1536
- +34 6 6039 6820

Min Cost= €8, No of Beds = 112, Facilities= KITCHEN, WASHING MACHINE, TUMBLE DRYER
Opening Times: 13:00 till 22:00. Open all year.

Private Rooms Os Chacotes

Complejo la Cabaña
- 42.87399, -7.85936
- +34 9 8238 0750
- complejolacabana@complejolacabana.com
- complejolacabana.com

♦=56€ ♦♦=75€

Restaurant has a good reputation.

Palas de Rei

68.1km to Santiago. 3.5km to San Xulián do Camiño. Altitude 554m. Local Facilities= CAFE/BAR, RESTAURANT, ATM, HOTEL OR GUEST HOUSE TYPE ACCOMMODATION, PHARMACY, MEDICAL CENTRE, GROCERY STORE. GPS: 42.87321, -7.86913

Notes on Palas de Rei

Palas de Rei has been a traditional overnight stay for pilgrims since the times of the Codex Calixtinus. Its name which means palace of the king relates to the palace built by the Visigoth king Witiza (702 to 710). There are no remains of this palace, and the oldest historic surviving building is the 12th century Romanesque Iglesia de San Tirso. This is the church which you walk right past on the Camino on your way into Palas de Rei. In terms of stamps, San Tirso claims the second oldest stamp on the Camino, only second in age to the final stamp at the pilgrim's office in Santiago. It also forms a meeting point for those without rooms when all accommodation is fully booked. If all accommodation is fully booked often the local councils will open up school buildings to house homeless pilgrims for the night. Whilst I personally dislike the loss of freedom by booking ahead, none the less at peak times it is advised to book your accommodation a couple of days in advance and for the Sarria to Santiago pilgrimage it is advised to book all your accommodation when you book your travel. Whilst on the subject of good advice, I have heard some pilgrims say that the Galicians are not very welcoming; I have to say that my experience has been the complete opposite and my advice concerning Galician hospitality is that when your host suggests moving on to the local Aguardente liquor called Orujo it is time to remember that you are on a pilgrimage, and it is definitely time for bed! Excess of Galician hospitality does not make for a great day's walking the following day!

When leaving Palas de Rei in the morning there are not many cafe/bars open for breakfast except for the cafe/bar Britania opposite the municipal albergue Xunta. Also, when leaving take a moment to look over the very pretty flowerbed made into the coat of arms of Palas de Rei.

Palas de Rei Town Map

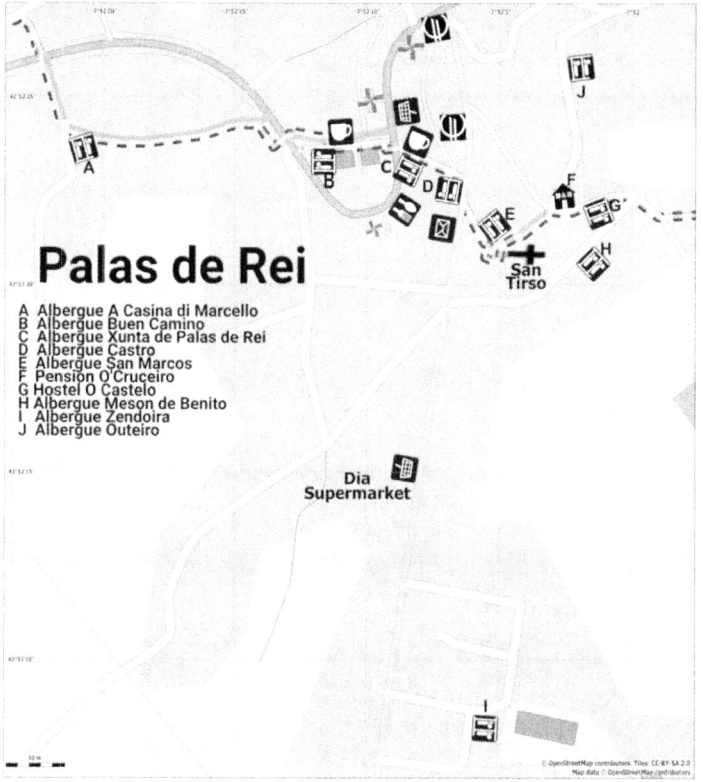

Palas de Rei

A Albergue A Casina di Marcello
B Albergue Buen Camino
C Albergue Xunta de Palas de Rei
D Albergue Castro
E Albergue San Marcos
F Pensión O'Cruceiro
G Hostel O Castelo
H Albergue Mesón de Benito
I Albergue Zendoira
J Albergue Outeiro

Dia Supermarket

Pilgrim Accommodation Palas do Rei

Albergue Xunta
- Avenida de Compostela, 19
- 42.87316, -7.86902
- +34 6 6039 6820
- +34 6 9991 2855

Min Cost= €8, No of Beds = 60, Facilities= KITCHEN, WASHING MACHINE, TUMBLE DRYER

Opening Times: 13:00 till 22:00. Open all year.

Albergue Mesón de Benito
- Rúa da Paz, S/N
- 42.87223, -7.86742
- +34 6 3683 4065
- +34 6 6723 2184
- info@alberguemesondebenito.com

🕸 alberguemesondebenito.com
Min Cost= €10, No of Beds = 100, Facilities= WASHING MACHINE, TUMBLE DRYER, WIFI
Opening Times: 12:00 till 00:00 Holy Week till October 31

Albergue San Marcos
- 📍 Travesía da Igrexa, 2
- 📍 42.87258, -7.86818
- ☎ +34 9 8238 0711
- ✉ info@alberguesanmarcos.es
- 🕸 alberguesanmarcos.com

Min Cost= €10, No of Beds = 71, Facilities= KITCHEN, WASHING MACHINE, TUMBLE DRYER, WIFI, PRIVATE ROOMS AVAILABLE
Opening Times: 11:00 till 23:00 March 1 till November 30

Albergue Outeiro
- 📍 Plaza de Galicia, 25
- 📍 42.87386, -7.86744
- ☎ +34 9 8238 0242
- ☎ +34 6 3013 4357
- ✉ info@albergueouteiro.com
- 🕸 www.albergueouteiro.com/en

Min Cost= €10, No of Beds = 50, Facilities= KITCHEN, WASHING MACHINE, TUMBLE DRYER, WIFI
Opening Times: 11:00 till 23:00 March 1 till October 31
🕸 www.booking.com/hotel/es/albergue-outeiro.html

Albergue Zendoira
- 📍 Rúa Amado Losada 10
- 📍 42.86905, -7.86826
- ☎ +34 6 0849 0075
- ✉ info@zendoira.com
- 🕸 zendoira.com

Min Cost= €10, No of Beds = 50, Facilities= KITCHEN, WASHING MACHINE, TUMBLE DRYER, WIFI, PRIVATE ROOMS AVAILABLE
Opening Times: 10:00. March 1 till October 31
🕸 www.booking.com/hotel/es/zendoira.html

Albergue Castro
- 📍 Avenida de Ourense, 24
- 📍 42.87297, -7.86843
- ☎ +34 9 8238 0321
- ☎ +34 6 0908 0655
- ✉ info@alberguecastro.com
- 🕸 alberguecastro.com

Min Cost= €10, No of Beds = 46, Facilities= WASHING MACHINE, TUMBLE DRYER
Opening Times: 10:00 till 23:00. Open all year.

Albergue Buen Camino
- 📍 Rúa do Peregrino, 3
- 📍 42.87321, -7.86983
- ☎ +34 9 8238 0233
- ☎ +34 6 3988 2229

albergebuencamino@yahoo.es
www.alberguebuencamino.com
Min Cost= €10, No of Beds = 41, Facilities= WASHING MACHINE, TUMBLE DRYER
Opening Times: 12:00 till 23:00 Holy Week till October 31

Albergue A Casiña di Marcello
- Calle Camiño de abaixo
- 42.87328, -7.87267
- +34 6 4072 3903
- alberguecasina@gmail.com
- www.albergueacasina.com

Min Cost= €10, No of Beds = 17, Facilities= KITCHEN, WASHING MACHINE, TUMBLE DRYER, WIFI COMMUNAL MEAL, PRIVATE ROOMS AVAILABLE
Opening Times: 14:00 till 22:00 March 1 till November 30
www.booking.com/hotel/es/albergue-a-casina-di-marcello.html

Private Rooms Palas de Rei

A Parada das Bestas
- 42.83046, -7.92234
- +34 9 8218 3614
- info@aparadadasbestas.com
- aparadadasbestas.com
- ♦=75€ ♦♦=75€

6.5km from Palas de Rei but has amazing reviews. Owners can arrange pickup and return to Palas de Rei.

Pensión As Hortas
- Rúa Hortas, 7
- 42.87380, -7.86954
- +34 6 2651 8388
- ♦=79€ ♦♦=79€

Hotel Casa Benilde
- Rúa do Mercado
- 42.87339, -7.86882
- +34 9 8238 0717
- hotelcasabenilde.com
- ♦=48€ ♦♦=77€

Pensión Casa Camiño
- Travesía Peregrino, 10
- 42.87330, -7.86995
- +34 9 8237 4066
- reservas@pulperiacasacamino.es
- www.pulperiacasacamino.es

👤=40€ 👤👤=55€
PensiónPalas.es
📍 42.87543, -7.86435
☎ +34 9 8238 0065 ☎ +34 6 6659 6044
✉ info@pensionpalas.es
🌐 www.pensionpalas.es
👤=50€ 👤👤=50€

About 400 metres out of town but has excellent reviews.

Casa Curro
📍 Avenida Ourense, 15   📍 42.87305, -7.86833
☎ +34 9 8238 0044
✉ info@casacurropalas.com
🌐 casacurropalas.com
👤=39€ 👤👤=58€

Chapter 6 - Palas de Rei to Arzúa

Waypoint Palas de Rei to Arzúa						
From	To	Decimal GPS	Distance	3.9 km/hr	4.6 km/hr	5.3 km/hr
Palas de Rei	San Xulián do Camiño	42.87451 -7.90333	3.5km	1hrs 0mins	0hrs 51mins	0hrs 44mins
San Xulián do Camiño	A Graña	42.87577 -7.90866	0.5km	0hrs 8mins	0hrs 6mins	0hrs 6mins
A Graña	Ponte Campaña	42.87847 -7.91439	0.5km	0hrs 9mins	0hrs 7mins	0hrs 6mins
Ponte Campaña	Casanova	42.87873 -7.92815	1.2km	0hrs 33mins	0hrs 28mins	0hrs 24mins
Casanova	Campanilla	42.88160 -7.95208	2.1km	0hrs 38mins	0hrs 33mins	0hrs 28mins
Campanilla	O Coto	42.88480 -7.95858	0.6km	0hrs 11mins	0hrs 9mins	0hrs 8mins
O Coto	Leboreiro	42.88770 -7.96556	0.6km	0hrs 10mins	0hrs 8mins	0hrs 7mins
Leboreiro	Furelos	42.90927 -7.99982	3.6km	1hrs 4mins	0hrs 54mins	0hrs 47mins
Furelos	Melide	42.91406 -8.01464	1.3km	0hrs 25mins	0hrs 21mins	0hrs 18mins
Melide	Parabispo	42.91544 -8.05716	4.1km	1hrs 14mins	1hrs 3mins	0hrs 55mins
Parabispo	Boente	42.91643 -8.07801	1.8km	0hrs 31mins	0hrs 26mins	0hrs 23mins
Boente	Castañeda	42.92592 -8.10414	2.7km	0hrs 49mins	0hrs 41mins	0hrs 36mins
Castañeda	Ribadiso da Baixo	42.93067 -8.13069	2.4km	0hrs 43mins	0hrs 37mins	0hrs 32mins
Ribadiso da Baixo	Arzúa	42.92662 -8.16248	3.2km	1hrs 1mins	0hrs 52mins	0hrs 45mins
Palas de Rei	Arzúa	42.92662 -8.16248	28.2km	8hrs 34mins	7hrs 16mins	6hrs 18mins

Palas de Rei to Arzúa Elevation Chart

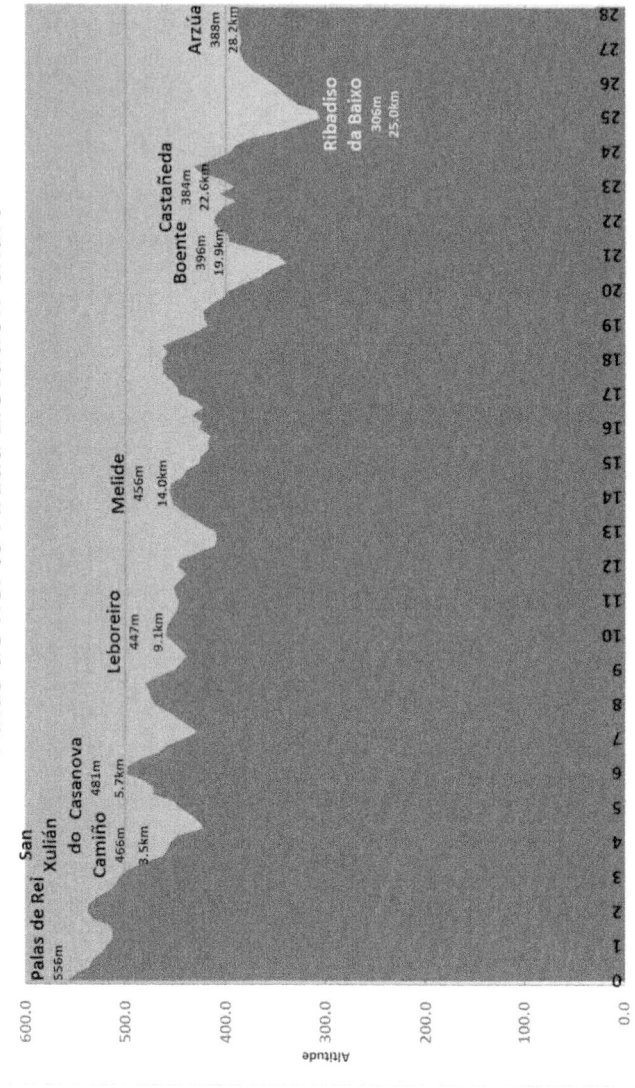

Location	Altitude	Distance
Palas de Rei	556m	
San Xulián do Camiño	481m	3.5km
Casanova	466m	5.7km
Leboreiro	447m	9.1km
Melide	456m	14.0km
Boente	396m	19.9km
Castañeda	384m	22.6km
Ribadiso da Baixo	306m	25.0km
Arzúa	388m	28.2km

89

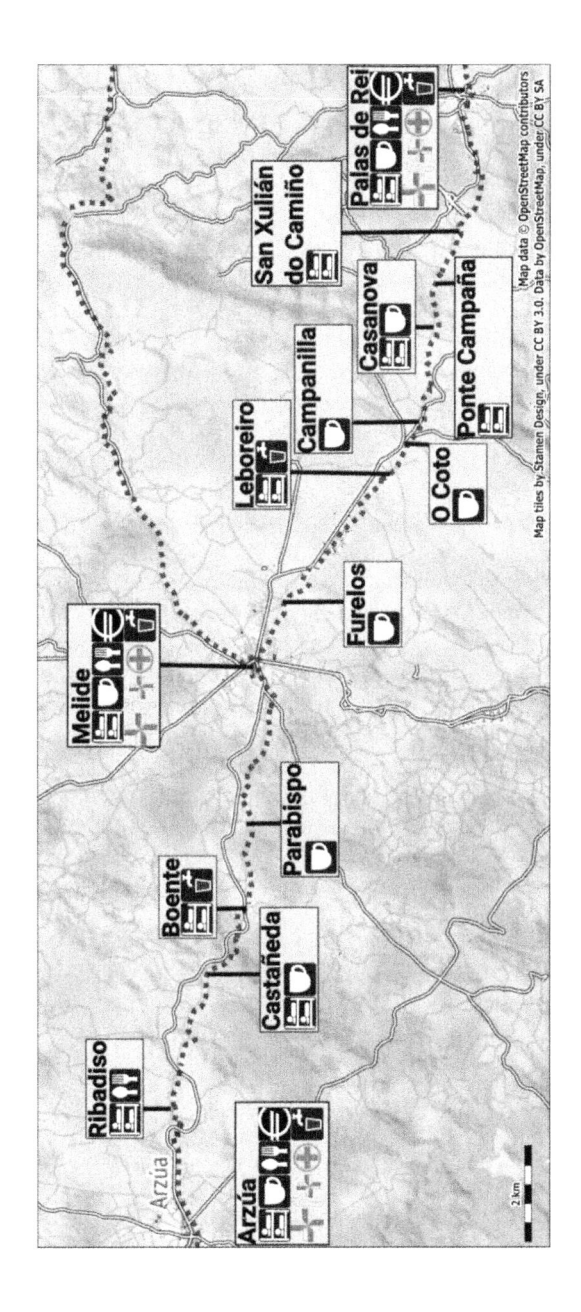

Notes about Today's Stage

At 28k today is the most demanding of your pilgrimage and involves about 8 and a half hours of walking plus breaks. Although overall you descend over 150 metres, you are frequently going up and downhill. This is the most demanding day which many of us choose to shorten slightly by staying in Ribadiso rather than making the full way to Arzúa. Some also choose to break this day in to two days by staying overnight in Melide, which is an option if you want to make a 6 day rather than a 5-day Camino.

The highlight of today is lunch in Melide which is reputed to have the best pulpo (octopus) in the whole of Galicia. Whether this is true or not I cannot say but I can say that the pulpo is very good. If octopus is not to your taste, then the restaurants do very good spit roast chicken and steaks as well. The Camino tradition is to have pulpo in A Garnacha (on the corner as you turn on to the high street) or Ezequiels (just further down the high street on the same side). The locals rate both restaurants as equally excellent, with Ezequiels being the more traditional of the two but my personal preference is for A Garnacha. If you are unsure about eating Octopus, there is usually a good selection of other dishes including Padron peppers, French fries, steak (in A Garnacha) and chicken (in Ezequiels). In A Garnacha the cheesecake is a truly exceptional dessert but remember you still have a long walk in the afternoon. There are plenty of opportunities for breaks every 4 or 5 kilometres today and I am a great believer that much of the magic of the Camino is worked when you sit down and share a drink and chat with people you have previously only said "buen camino" to along the way.

San Xulián do Camiño

64.7km to Santiago. 0.5km to A Graña. Altitude 467m. Local Facilities= Café/Bar. GPS: 42.87444, -7.90321

Notes on San Xulián do Camiño

The story of Saint Julian the Hospitaller is a strange but apt story for the Camino in that Saint Julian uses pilgrimage and hospitality to pilgrims to atone for his terrible sin of killing his parents. Before telling the story, it is worth noting that Saint Julian is the patron saint of the following: boatmen, carnival workers, childless people, circus workers, clowns, ferrymen, fiddle players, hospitallers, hotelkeepers, hunters, innkeepers, jugglers, wandering musicians, knights, murderers, pilgrims, shepherds, travellers and, in of particular interest to us pilgrims, to obtain lodging while traveling.

The story of Saint Julian starts with the night of his birth in Le Mans, France when his father witnessed pagan witches curse his son into killing both his parents. His father wanted to get rid of the child, but his mother would not let him do so. As Julian grew up he found out about the curse (some legends tell that he was told of the curse by a stag while out hunting). Julian decided he would prevent the curse from ever happening by leaving home and moving far away. After walking 50 days Julian reached Galicia and settled down with a good wife. Some twenty years later his parents made a pilgrimage to Santiago. While Julian was out hunting, Julian's wife not knowing his parents put up the two tired old pilgrims in her own bed. Upon his return, Julian came across the couple in his marital bed and believing them to be his wife with a lover he murdered both of them in a fit of rage. When he realised his mistake, Julian was horrified by what he had done but his wife consoled him and told him to trust in Christ's forgiveness and persuaded him to atone by making a pilgrimage to Rome. After this pilgrimage, Saint Julian set up several pilgrim hostels and dedicated his life to caring for pilgrims on their pilgrimage and in this way gradually atoned for his terrible sin.

San Xulián do Camiño Village Map

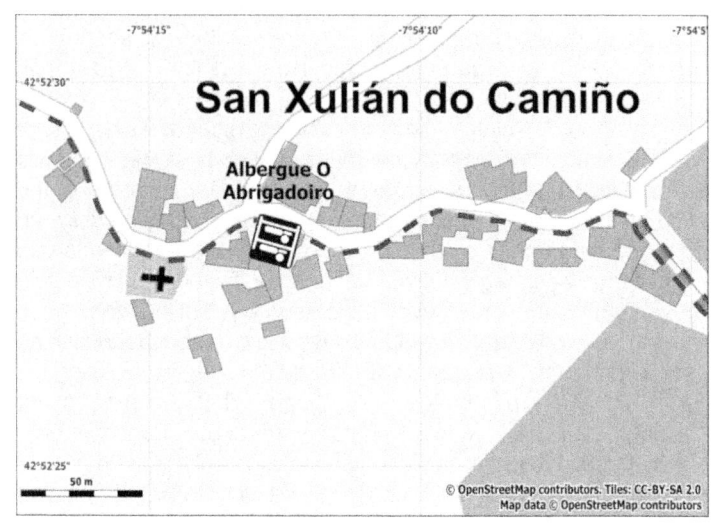

Pilgrim Accommodation San Xulián do Camiño

Albergue O Abrigadoiro
✆ 42.87447, -7.9035 ☏ +34 6 7659 6975
✉ oabrigadoiro1@gmail.com
Min Cost= €12, No of Beds = 12, Facilities= WASHING MACHINE, TUMBLE DRYER, WIFI, COMMUNAL MEAL
Opening Times: 12:00 till 23:00 Holy Week till October 31
Lovely small rural albergue.

A Graña

64.2km to Santiago. 0.5km to Casanova. Altitude 455m. Local Facilities= Café/Bar. GPS: 42.87577, -7.90866

Notes on A Graña

A small bar with a nice B&B attached.

Private Rooms A Graña

La Pallota de San Cristóbal
✆ 42.87577, -7.90866
☏ +34 6 5907 0510 ☏ +34 6 7363 4476

✉ lapallotadesancristobal@gmail.com
🌐 www.lapallotasancristobal.com
👤=80€ 👥=80€

Ponte Campaña

63.6km to Santiago. 1.2km to Casanova. Altitude 422m. Local Facilities= NONE. GPS: 42.87838, -7.91440

Notes on Ponte Campaña

Watch out for the huge shell on the Albergue Casa Domingo just after you pass the small bridge over the Río Pambre.

Pilgrim Accommodation Ponte Campaña

Albergue Casa Domingo
📍 42.87807, -7.91453
☎ +34 9 8216 3226   ☎ +34 6 3072 8864
✉ info@alberguecasadomingo.com
🌐 www.alberguecasadomingo.com
Min Cost= €10, No of Beds = 18, Facilities= WASHING MACHINE, TUMBLE DRYER, WIFI, COMMUNAL MEAL
Opening Times: 12:00 till 23:00 Holy Week till October 31

Casanova

62.4km to Santiago. 2.1km to Campanilla. Altitude 482m. Local Facilities= Café/bar. GPS: 42.87873, -7.92828

Notes on Casanova

There used to be three café/bars in Casanova but the pandemic has reduced this to just one which is a good café/bar at the entrance of Casanova.

Please note that the Casa Rural Bolboreta is an excellent B&B and will generally pick you up in Casanova, if you fancy staying there but resent the extra distance off-Camino you would have to walk.

Ponte Campaña / Casanova Village Map

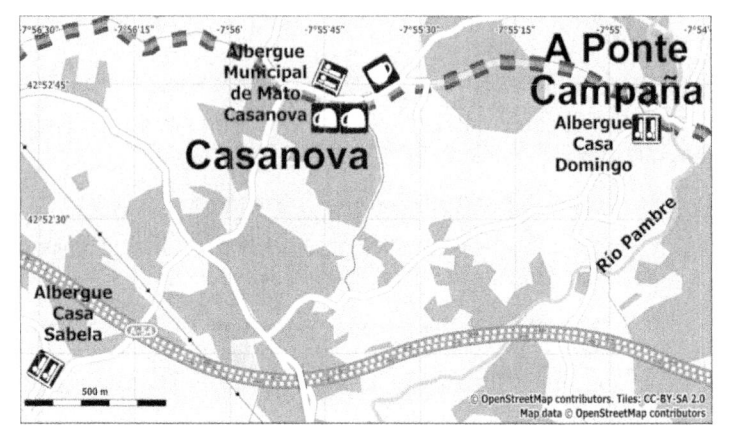

Pilgrim Accommodation Casanova

Albergue Xunta
- O Mato, Casanova
- +34 6 6039 6821
- 42.87883, -7.92894
- +34 6 3896 2803

Min Cost= €8, No of Beds = 20, Facilities= WASHING MACHINE, TUMBLE DRYER
Opening Times: 13:00 till 22:00. Open all year.

Private Rooms Casanova

Casa Rural Bolboreta
- 42.86992, -7.94101
- +34 6 0912 4717
- ♦=60€ ♦♦=85€
- www.booking.com/hotel/es/a-bolboreta.html

Campanilla

60.3km to Santiago. 0.6km to O Coto. Altitude 466m. Local Facilities= CAFE/BAR. GPS: 42.8816, -7.95208

O Coto

59.7km to Santiago. 0.6km to Leboreiro. Altitude 478m. Local Facilities= CAFE/BAR, HOTEL OR GUEST HOUSE TYPE ACCOMMODATION. GPS: 42.8848, -7.95858

Private Rooms O Coto

Casa de los Somoza

📍 42.88487, -7.95892
☎ +34 9 8150 7372
✉ infocasadelossomoza@gmail.com
🌐 casadelossomoza.com
🚹=70€ 🚹🚹=70€
Excellent café bar.

Los Dos Alemanes

📍 42.88520, -7.95698
☎ +34 6 3091 0803
✉ estefaniaoteropazos@gmail.com
🌐 los-dos-alemanes.webnode.es
🚹=70€ 🚹🚹=70€

Leboreiro

59.1km to Santiago. 3.6km to Furelos. Altitude 447m. Local Facilities= NONE. GPS: 42.88799, -7.96560

Notes on Leboreiro

Leboreiro is also mentioned in the Codex Calixtinus but not in subsequent guides and we can only assume its importance diminished. Of note in Leboreiro is the 13th century gothic church of Santa María de Leboreiro which although technically Gothic has several Romanesque features. On the outside above the entrance is a beautiful engraving of the Virgin and Child (this type of image above the entrance to a church is called a tympanum). There is a legend associated with this engraving. The legend goes that the villages noticed a strange light and a beautiful fragrance coming from a nearby fountain. Suspecting a miracle, the villagers started digging around the fountain and uncovered an image of the Virgin. They took the image back to the church and placed it on the altar. However, the Virgin was not happy with this and the image returned to the fountain at night. The following day the villagers reclaimed the image and bought it back to the church. This transporting of the image of the Virgin carried on for a few days until a local sculptor had the idea of sculpting an image of the Virgin on the tympanum and rededicating the church to the Virgin. After which the image of the Virgin was happy to remain in the church. Inside the church is a 14th century statue of the Virgin and a 16th century painted mural which depicts the visitation of Saint Elizabeth to the Virgin, the flagellation of Christ and the martyrdom of San Sebastián.

Furelos

55.5km to Santiago. 1.3km to Melide. Altitude 409m. Local Facilities= CAFE/BAR, HOTEL OR GUEST HOUSE TYPE ACCOMMODATION. GPS: 42.90926, -7.99994

Private Rooms Furelos

Casa Adro
✆ 42.90874, -7.99885
☏ +34 6 1667 8206
⌂ casaadro.com
👤=85€ 👥=85€
Excellent reviews.

Notes on Furelos

This village was once run by the Order of Knights of the Hospital of Saint John of Jerusalem (whose emblem is a Maltese Cross). They are also known as the Knights Hospitaller and had a dual role of caring for the sick and the protection of pilgrims. There is little left of the pilgrim hospital they once ran here and even the 13th century church of San Juan has been heavily remodelled in the 1920s in a neogothic style leaving little of the original church visible. The medieval bridge, however, is probably the best of the many bridges on the Camino through Galicia and is one my favourite spots for taking photographs.

Melide

54.2km to Santiago. 4.1km to Parabispo. Altitude 456m. Local Facilities= CAFE/BAR, RESTAURANT, ATM, HOTEL OR GUEST HOUSE TYPE ACCOMMODATION, PHARMACY, MEDICAL CENTRE, GROCERY STORE. GPS: 42.91389, -8.01473

Notes on Melide

There has been a settlement around Melide since Neolithic times. In Roman times, it was the crossing point of two major

Roman roads, the Via Trajana and the road to the province of Cantabria. But much of its growth and status in the middle ages are owed to its position on both the Camino Francés and the Camino Primitivo (which starts in Oviedo).

Melide is a big, busy and modern town but has several buildings of note including the present chapel of San Pedro and San Roque, located on the corner of San Roque, built in 1949 with materials from the two demolished medieval churches of San Pedro and San Roque. Its beautiful entrance comes from the old Romanesque church of San Pedro. Inside the retablo (altarpiece) dates from the nineteenth century, with the central image being of San Roque. Also, inside are various 14th century tombs. Outside is one of the oldest cruceiros (stone crosses) on the Camino which is thought to date from the 14th century. The front depicts Christ sitting in Glory showing his wounded hands, the rear depicts Christ's suffering on the cross.

The church of Sancti Spiritus, in the Plaza del Convento, was part of the monastery of the Third Order of St. Francis which was founded in the fourteenth century. Of this 14th century church all that remains is a small side chapel. In 1498, Sancho Sanchez de Ulloa decided to rebuild the convent church in memory of his mother Ines de Castro using the stone from the remains of the castle.

There is daily mass at 17:30h (except in July and August when mass is at 18:00h) in the Capilla del Carmen on the way out of Melide along the Camino in Rúa Principal. This chapel was built in 1741, on the site where the medieval castle of Melide had once stood.

My favourite church in Melide is the 12th century Romanesque Iglesia de Santa Maria which is about 5 minutes out of town just by what used to be the 50km marker (which is now the 51.629 km marker) that is the front cover to this book. Recently, a guide has been in attendance in the afternoons to give pilgrims a guided tour of this charming chapel in return for a small donation. This chapel and its beautiful Romanesque retablo (altarpiece) is dedicated to Our Lady of the Snows.

Melide

- A Hostel Montoto
- B Albergue de Melide
- C Albergue Turistico O Apalpador
- D Albergue San Antón
- E Albergue Vilela
- F Albergue Pereiro
- G Albergue O Cruceiro
- H Albergue O Apalpador II
- I Pulpería Ezequiel
- J Pulpeira A Garnacha
- K Albergue Ezequiel

Pilgrim Accommodation Melide

Albergue Xunta
- Rúa San Antonio
- +34 6 5958 2931
- 42.91447, -8.01819
- +34 6 4993 1348

Min Cost= €8, No of Beds = 156, Facilities= KITCHEN, WASHING MACHINE, TUMBLE DRYER
Opening Times: 13:00 till 22:00. Open all year.

Albergue Turistico O Apalpador
- Rúa San Antonio, 23
- +34 9 8150 6266
- 42.91458, -8.01791
- +34 6 7983 7969
- jose_morata69@hotmail.com
- www.albergueoapalpador.com

Min Cost= €10, No of Beds = 54, Facilities= KITCHEN, WASHING MACHINE, TUMBLE DRYER, WIFI
Opening Times: 11:00 till 23:00. Open all year.

Albergue Pereiro
- Rúa Progreso, 43
- +34 9 8150 6314
- 42.91315, -8.01736
- info@alberguepereiro.com
- www.alberguepereiro.com

Min Cost= €10, No of Beds = 45, Facilities= KITCHEN, WASHING MACHINE, TUMBLE DRYER, WIFI, PRIVATE ROOMS AVAILABLE
Opening Times: 11:00 till 23:00. Open all year.
- www.booking.com/hotel/es/hostel-pereiro.html

Albergue Melide
- Avenida Lugo, 92
- +34 6 2790 1552
- 42.91241, -8.00666
- info@alberguemelide.com
- www.alberguemelide.com

Min Cost= €10, No of Beds = 42, Facilities= KITCHEN,
Opening Times: 11:00 till 23:00 Holy Week till October 31

Hostel Montoto
- Rúa Codeseira, 31
- +34 9 8150 7337
- 42.91252, -8.01911
- +34 6 4694 1887
- alberguemontoto@gmail.com
- www.alberguemontoto.com

Min Cost= €12, No of Beds = 42, Facilities= KITCHEN, WASHING MACHINE, TUMBLE DRYER, WIFI, PRIVATE ROOMS AVAILABLE

Opening Times: 11:00 till 23:00 Holy Week till October 31
🕸 www.booking.com/hotel/es/albergue-montoto.html

Albergue San Anton
- Rúa San Antonio, 6
- 42.91475, -8.01710
- ☎ +34 9 8150 6427
- ☎ +34 6 9815 3672
- ✉ alberguesananton@gmail.com
- 🕸 www.alberguesananton.com

Min Cost= €12, No of Beds = 36, Facilities= KITCHEN, WASHING MACHINE, TUMBLE DRYER, WIFI, PRIVATE ROOMS AVAILABLE
Opening Times: 10:30 till 23:00 March 1 till November 30
🕸 www.booking.com/hotel/es/albergue-san-anton.html

Albergue Alfonso II
- Avenida Toques e Friol, 52
- 42.91824, -8.01469
- ☎ +34 9 8150 6454
- ☎ +34 6 0860 4850
- ✉ info@alberguealfonsoelcasto.com
- 🕸 www.alberguealfonsoelcasto.com

Min Cost= €10, No of Beds = 34, Facilities= KITCHEN, WASHING MACHINE, TUMBLE DRYER, WIFI
Opening Times: 11:30 till 23:00 March 1 till October 31

Albergue Arraigos
- Cantón de San Roque, 9 Entreplanta
- 42.91389, -8.01389
- ☎ +34 6 0088 0769
- ☎ +34 8 8197 8663
- ✉ alberguearraigos@gmail.com

Min Cost= €10, No of Beds = 20, Facilities= KITCHEN, WASHING MACHINE, TUMBLE DRYER, WIFI
Opening Times: 11:00 till 00:00. Open all year.

Albergue O Cruceiro
- Ronda de A Coruña, 2
- 42.9141, -8.01471
- ☎ +34 6 1676 4896
- ✉ info@alberguecocruceiro.es
- 🕸 www.albergueocruceiro.es/index.php/en

Min Cost= €10, No of Beds = 72, Facilities= KITCHEN, WASHING MACHINE, TUMBLE DRYER, WIFI
Opening Times: 11:00 till 23:00 Holy Week till October 31

Albergue O Candil
- Rúa Principal, 21
- 42.91414, -8.017
- ☎ +34 6 3950 3550
- ✉ info@ocandil.gal
- 🕸 www.ocandil.gal/es

Min Cost= €15, No of Beds = 12, Facilities= KITCHEN, WASHING MACHINE, TUMBLE DRYER, WIFI, PRIVATE ROOMS AVAILABLE
Opening Times: 12:00 till 21:00 March 15 till October 15
🕸 www.booking.com/hotel/es/albergue-o-candil.html

Albergue Ezequiel
- Rúa Sol, 7   42.91312, -8.01255
- ☎ +34 6 8658 3378
- 🕸 www.pulperiaezequiel.com/albergue-melide.html

Min Cost= €10, No of Beds = 19, Facilities= KITCHEN, WASHING MACHINE, TUMBLE DRYER, WIFI PRIVATE ROOMS AVAILABLE
Opening Times: 13:00 till 23:00. Open all year.

Private Rooms Melide

Pensión San Anton
- Rúa San Antonio, 14   42.91471, -8.01750
- ☎ +34 6 0161 9618
- ✉ pensionsananton@gmail.com
- 🕸 pensionsananton.com
- 👤=35€ 👤👤👤=80€

Outdoor swimming pool, A/C & great reviews.

Pension Ferradura
- Rúa Luis Seoane, 8   42.91126, -8.01478
- ☎ +34 6 0165 0660
- 🕸 pension-ferradura.negocio.site
- 👤=63€ 👤👤=70€

Hotel Restaurante Xaneiro
- Avenida Habana,43   42.91471, -8.01153
- ☎ +34 9 8150 6140
- ✉ hotel@xaneiro.com
- 🕸 xaneiro.com
- 👤=45€ 👤👤=45€

A Lúa do Camiño
- Rúa Circunvalación, 15   42.91164, -8.00774
- ☎ +34 6 2095 8331
- ✉ luadocamino@gmail.com
- 👤=30€ 👤👤=35€

Outdoor swimming pool & excellent reviews.

Hotel Restaurante Carlos

- Avenida de Lugo, 119   - 42.91228, -8.00503
- ☏ +34 9 8150 7633
- gestion@hc96.com
- www.hc96.com
- ♂=27€ ♂♂=35€

Notes on the route from Melide to Boente

At the 50.521 (GPS: 42.91283, -8.03759) marker there is a complementary route to the left which goes through the hamlet of Penas. The recommended route is the direct and very pretty direct / right route but involves going over a beautiful steppingstone bridge over the river Catasol. This bridge can be a fabulous photo opportunity but equally can be daunting. If it is dark or you are not fully confident, you may well prefer the complementary route.

Parabispo

50.0km to Santiago. 1.8km to Boente. Altitude 458m. Local Facilities= CAFE/BAR. GPS: 42.91543, -8.05716

Boente

48.2km to Santiago. 2.7km to Castañeda. Altitude 396m. Local Facilities=CAFE/BAR. GPS: 42.91620, -8.07801

Notes on Boente

The church of Santiago de Boente is a 20th century church but generally is left open and provides the opportunity to get 5 minutes of calm and coolness on a sweltering day as well as a stamp.

The fountain next to the stone cross in Boente called the Fonte de Saleta (the fountain of health) is said to have curative powers. In my experience, any water fountain on a sweltering day has curative powers.

Boente Village Map

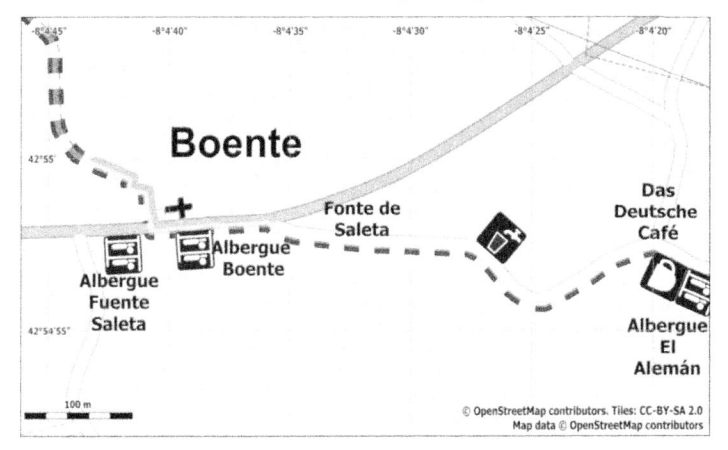

Pilgrim Accommodation Boente

Albergue Boente
- Boente – Arzúa
- +34 9 8150 1974
- info@albergueboente.com
- 42.91608, -8.07751
- +34 6 3832 1707
- albergueboente.com

Min Cost= €12, No of Beds = 40, Facilities= WASHING MACHINE, TUMBLE DRYER, WIFI, SWIMMING POOL, PRIVATE ROOMS AVAILABLE
Opening Times: 12:00 till 23:00 March 1 till November 30
www.booking.com/hotel/es/albergue-boente-boente.html

Albergue Fuente Saleta
- Boente – Arzúa
- +34 9 8150 1853
- fuentesaleta@hotmail.com
- www.facebook.com/albergue.fuentesaleta
- 42.91587, -8.0782
- +34 6 4883 6213

Min Cost= €12, No of Beds = 22, Facilities= WASHING MACHINE, TUMBLE DRYER, WIFI
Opening Times: 11:00 till 23:00 March 1 till November 30

Albergue El Alemán
- Lugar Boente Arriba
- +34 9 8150 1984
- info@albergueelaleman.com
- 42.9158, -8.07186
- +34 6 7725 1300

www.alberguelaleman.com
Min Cost= €12, No of Beds = 40, Facilities= WASHING MACHINE, TUMBLE DRYER, WIFI, SWIMMING POOL
Opening Times: 12:00 till 19:00 March 15 till October 30

Castañeda

45.6km to Santiago. 2.4km to Ribadiso da Baixo. Altitude 383m. Local Facilities= CAFE/BAR. GPS: 42.92607, -8.10416

Notes on Castañeda

In medieval times pilgrims were asked to carry limestone from Triacastela (about 25km before Sarria) to Castañeda where it would be slaked in the ovens and used in the construction of the cathedral at Santiago.

Castañeda Village Map

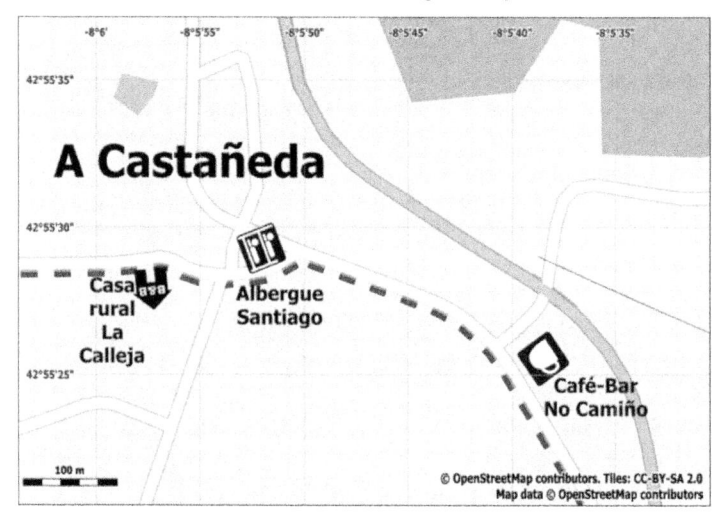

Pilgrim Accommodation Castañeda

Albergue Bar Santiago
- Castañeda
- +34 9 8150 1711
- albergue.santiago.castaneda@gmail.com
- 42.92476, -8.0974
- +34 6 9976 1698

Min Cost= €11, No of Beds = 6, Facilities= WASHING MACHINE, TUMBLE DRYER, WIFI, PRIVATE ROOMS AVAILABLE
Opening Times: 12:00 till N/A. Open all year.

Ribadiso da Baixo

43.1km to Santiago. 3.2km to Arzúa. Altitude 306m. Local Facilities= CAFE/BAR, RESTAURANT. GPS: 42.93068, -8.13063

Notes on Ribadiso da Baixo

The municipal (Xunta) albergue in Ribadiso backs onto the river next to the bridge. On hot days the river provides a lovely opportunity to paddle and cool your feet. This municipal albergue built in 1993 is on the original site of one of the medieval pilgrim hostels. If accommodation is available, Ribadiso provides a more relaxing location to spend the night than Arzúa. Though Arzúa provides more opportunities to enjoy the great local cheese.

Ribadiso da Baixo Village Map

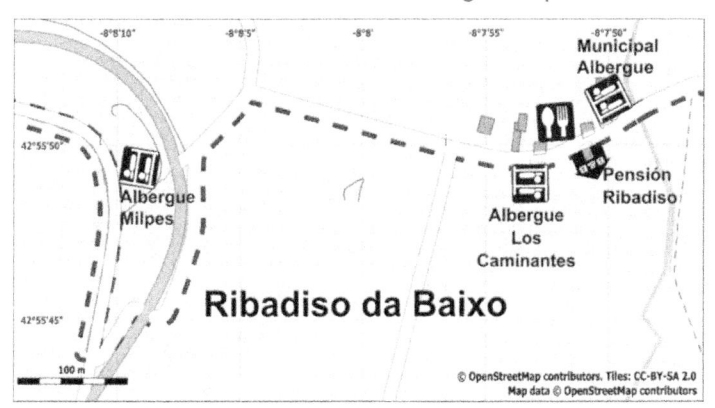

Pilgrim Accommodation Ribadiso da Baixo

Albergue Xunta
- Ribadiso de Abaixo, s/n
- 42.930872, -8.130525
- +34 6 6039 6823
- +34 6 3896 2801

Min Cost= €8, No of Beds = 70, Facilities= KITCHEN, WASHING MACHINE, TUMBLE DRYER
Opening Times: 13:00 till 22:00. Open all year.

Albergue Los Caminantes
- Ribadiso de Abaixo, s/n
- 42.93042, -8.1314
- +34 6 4702 0600
- info@albergueloscaminantes.com
- www.ribadiso.albergueloscaminantes.com

Min Cost= €10, No of Beds = 56, Facilities= KITCHEN, WASHING MACHINE, TUMBLE DRYER, WIFI, PRIVATE ROOMS AVAILABLE
Opening Times: 12:00 till 22:30 Holy Week till October 31
- www.booking.com/hotel/es/pension-albergue-los-caminantes.html

Albergue Milpes
- Ribadiso de Arriba, 7
- 42.93045, -8.13611
- +34 9 8150 0425
- +34 6 1665 2276
- alberguemilpes@gmail.com
- www.alberguemilpes.com

Min Cost= €12, No of Beds = 28, Facilities= WASHING MACHINE, TUMBLE DRYER, WIFI
Opening Times: 11:00 till 23:00. March thru October.
- www.booking.com/hotel/es/albergue-milpes.es.html

Probably one of the best albergues on the whole Camino Francés, the owner, Aitor, is a bathroom fitter by trade and as a consequence the shared bathrooms are excellent.

Albergue Mirador de Ribadiso
- Ribadiso de Arriba, 8
- 42.93048, -8.13633
- +34 7 2229 7498

Min Cost= €12, No of Beds = 10, Facilities= WASHING MACHINE, TUMBLE DRYER, WIFI, PRIVATE ROOMS AVAILABLE
Opening Times: 11:00 till 23:00. Open all year.

Private Rooms Ribadiso

Pensión Ribadiso
- 42.93058, -8.13085
- +34 6 6913 1955
- ♂=59€ ♂♂=59€

Swimming pool & great reputation.

Arzúa

39.9km to Santiago. 2.3km to Pregontoño. Altitude 387m. Local Facilities= CAFE/BAR, RESTAURANT, ATM, HOTEL OR GUEST

HOUSE TYPE ACCOMMODATION, PHARMACY, MEDICAL CENTRE, GROCERY STORE. GPS: 42.92634, -8.16262

Notes on Arzúa

The major disadvantage of staying at Ribadiso, as I normally choose to do, is that I pass through Arzúa early in the morning while all the shops that sell the wonderful local cheese are still closed. As you may have guessed I am a huge fan of the local cheese, which by the way is excellent toasted and very good on burgers. On my bucket list is to attend the cheese festival in Arzúa which is held the first weekend in March each year (www.festadoqueixo.org). The importance of cheese to Arzúa can also be seen in the statue in the main square which is dedicated to "La Queixeira" (the cheese maker) (42.92673, -8.16378).

In Arzúa you may be joined by pilgrims who have walked the Camino del Norte (which goes across Spain's northern coast) as the two Caminos merge.

Although the Iglesia de Santiago (42.92632, -8.16340) was rebuilt in the 1950s, it houses three impressive retablos (altarpieces). The main altarpiece dates from the 19th century and has at its top a depiction of Saint James intervening in the mythical battle of Clavijo. The 18th-century Rococo altarpiece of the north aisle is dedicated to Our Lady of Mount Carmel. Made in 1779 and painted in 1792 by José Edrosa the altarpiece of the Rosary located in the south aisle is the most impressive. At the centre it has an image of Our Lady of the Most Holy Rosary with Christ depicted as a child standing on a globe. The image at the top is San Roque, the patron saint invoked in times of disease or pestilence. To the left is the statue of the patron saint of farmers and labourers, Saint Isidore and to the right is the statue of Saint Raymond Nonnatus, patron saint of childbirth, midwives, children, pregnant women, and priests who want to protect the secrecy of confession. Mass is said daily in the church at 19:00h.

Also, of note is La Capilla de la Magdalena (42.92627, -8.16287) which was founded in the sixteenth century by the Augustinian Friars who created a small hospital to welcome the pilgrims. The chapel has a single rectangular nave, over the door is semi-circular arch on the facade, which reveals its Romanesque style. There are plans to turn this chapel into a small museum.

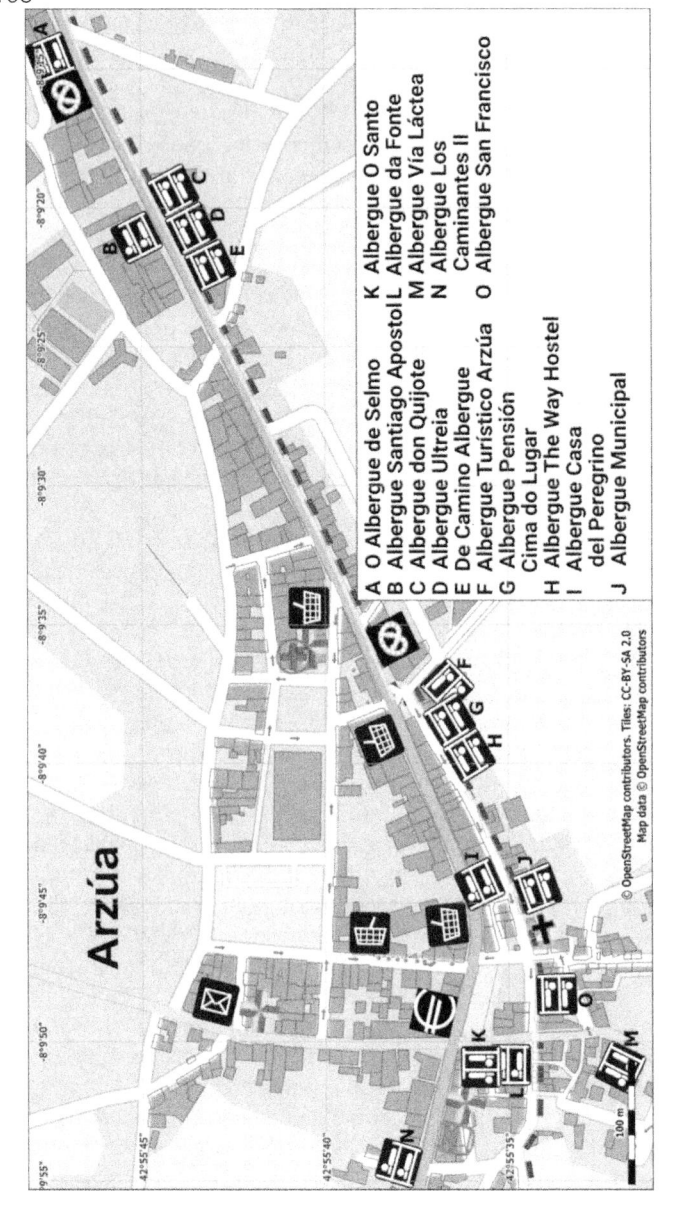

Arzúa

- A Albergue de Selmo
- B Albergue Santiago Apostol
- C Albergue don Quijote
- D Albergue Ultreia
- E De Camino Albergue
- F Albergue Turístico Arzúa
- G Albergue Pensión Cima do Lugar
- H Albergue The Way Hostel
- I Albergue Casa del Peregrino
- J Albergue Municipal
- K Albergue O Santo
- L Albergue da Fonte
- M Albergue Vía Láctea
- N Albergue Los Caminantes II
- O Albergue San Francisco

Pilgrim Accommodation Arzúa

Albergue Xunta
- Cima do Lugar, 6
- +34 6 6039 6824
- 42.926219, -8.162726
- +34 6 3896 2800

Min Cost= €8, No of Beds = 50, Facilities= KITCHEN, WASHING MACHINE, TUMBLE DRYER
Opening Times: 13:00 till 22:00. Open all year.

Albergue Vía Lactea
- Calle José Neira Vilas, 26
- +34 9 8150 0581
- 42.92546, -8.16414
- +34 6 1675 9447
- info@alberguevialactea.com
- www.alberguevialactea.com

Min Cost= €14, No of Beds = 60, Facilities= KITCHEN, WASHING MACHINE, TUMBLE DRYER, WIFI
Opening Times: 12:00 till 23:00. Open all year.
- www.booking.com/hotel/es/albergue-via-lactea-arzua.html

Albergue Los Caminantes II
- Rúa de Santiago, 14
- +34 6 4702 0600
- 42.92714, -8.16511
- info@alberguelocaminantes.com
- www.arzua.alberguelocaminantes.com

Min Cost= €10, No of Beds = 60, Facilities= KITCHEN, WASHING MACHINE, TUMBLE DRYER, WIFI
Opening Times: 11:00 till 22:30 Holy Week till October 31

O Albergue de Selmo
- Rúa Lugo, 133
- +34 9 8193 9018
- 42.92976, -8.15407
- info@oalberguedeselmo.com
- oalberguedeselmo.com

Min Cost= €12, No of Beds = 50, Facilities= KITCHEN, WASHING MACHINE, TUMBLE DRYER, WIFI
Opening Times: 12:00 till 22:30 May 1 till October 31

De Camino Albergue
- Avenida de Lugo, 118
- +34 9 8150 0415
- 42.92867, -8.15616
- info@decaminoalbergue.com
- www.decaminoalbergue.com

Min Cost= €12, No of Beds = 42, Facilities= WASHING MACHINE, TUMBLE DRYER, WIFI
Opening Times: 12:00 till 22:00 February 1 till November 30
www.booking.com/hotel/es/de-camino.html

Albergue Ultreia
- Rúa Lugo, 126
- 42.92889, -8.15571
- +34 9 8150 0471
- +34 6 2663 9450
- info@albergueultreia.com
- www.albergueultreia.com

Min Cost= €10, No of Beds = 39, Facilities= KITCHEN, WASHING MACHINE, TUMBLE DRYER, WIFI
Opening Times: 12:00 till 23:30. Open all year.
www.booking.com/hotel/es/albergue-ultreia.html

Hostel Cruce de Caminos Arzúa
- Rúa Cima do Lugar, 28
- 42.92698, -8.16085
- +34 8 8181 7716
- +34 6 0405 1353
- recepciondecaminos@gmail.com
- www.crucedecaminosarzua.com

Min Cost= €14, No of Beds = 36, Facilities= WIFI
Opening Times: 12:00 till 20:00 April 1 till October 31
www.booking.com/hotel/es/the-way-hostel-arzua.html

Albergue Turístico Arzúa
- Rúa Rosalía de Castro, 2
- 42.9271, -8.16037
- +34 9 8150 8233
- +34 6 0838 0011
- pensionarzua@gmail.com
- www.facebook.com/Albergue-Turístico-Arzúa-1868225773466047

Min Cost= €10, No of Beds = 12, Facilities= KITCHEN, WASHING MACHINE, TUMBLE DRYER, WIFI
Opening Times: 12:00 till 22:00 February 1 till November 30

Albergue A Conda
- Rúa da Calexa, 92
- 42.93282, -8.15972
- +34 9 8150 0068
- +34 6 8792 6604
- hosvilarino@gmail.com
- www.pensionvilarino.com

Min Cost= €10, No of Beds = 18, Facilities= WIFI, PRIVATE ROOMS AVAILABLE
Opening Times: No check-in restrictions. March 1 till November 30

Albergue Casa del Peregrino
- Calle Cima do Lugar, 7
- 42.92644, -8.16237
- +34 6 8670 8704
- www.facebook.com/anabelenvv

Min Cost= €12, No of Beds = 14, Facilities= KITCHEN, WASHING MACHINE, TUMBLE DRYER, WIFI
Opening Times: 12:00 till 22:00 April 1 till October 31

Albergue Pensión Cima do Lugar
- Calle Cima do Lugar, 22
- 42.92705, -8.16066
- +34 9 8150 0559
- +34 6 6163 3669
- acimadolugar@gmail.com

Min Cost= €12, No of Beds = 14, Facilities= KITCHEN, WASHING MACHINE, TUMBLE DRYER, WIFI
Opening Times: 11:30 till 22:30. Open all year.
- www.booking.com/hotel/es/albergue-pension-cima-do-lugar.html

Albergue Santiago Apóstol
- Avenida de Lugo, 107
- 42.92918, -8.15556
- +34 9 8150 8132
- +34 6 6042 7771
- santiagoapostolalbergue@hotmail.com
- www.alberguesantiagoapostol.com

Min Cost= €12, No of Beds = 72, Facilities= KITCHEN, WASHING MACHINE, TUMBLE DRYER, WIFI
Opening Times: 12:00 till 23:00. Open all year.

Albergue San Francisco
- Rúa do Carme, 7
- 42.92618, -8.1636
- +34 8 8197 9304
- +34 6 0406 9338
- info@alberguesanfrancisco.com
- alberguesanfrancisco.com

Min Cost= €14, No of Beds = 28, Facilities= KITCHEN, WASHING MACHINE, TUMBLE DRYER, WIFI
Opening Times: 12:00 till 21:30 March 1 till November 30

Private Rooms Arzúa

1930 Boutique Hotel
- Rúa das Dores, 19
- 42.92581, -8.16375
- +34 6 7078 4787
- info@1930boutiquehotel.com

🏠 www.1930boutiquehotel.com
👤=70€ 👥=93€

Hotel Arzúa
- 📞 Calle Lugo 132
- ☎ +34 9 8150 0681
- ✉ info@hotelarzua.com
- 🏠 www.hotelarzua.com
- 📞 42.92917, -8.15506
- ☎ +34 6 8996 9996

👤=60€ 👥=60€

Pensión Casa Teodora
- 📞 Calle Lugo 38
- ☎ +34 9 8150 0083
- ✉ reservas@casateodora.com
- 🏠 www.casateodora.com
- 📞 42.92712, -8.16088

👤=55€ 👥=55€

Pensión Casa Frade
- 📞 Rúa de Ramón Franco, 10
- ☎ +34 9 8150 0019
- 📞 42.92726, -8.16388

👤=38€ 👥=52€

Old fashioned, family run.

Casa Carballeira
- 📞 Rúa de Ramón Franco, 14
- ☎ +34 9 8150 0094
- ✉ casacarballeiraarzua@gmail.com
- 🏠 casacarballeiraarzua.com
- 📞 42.92742, -8.16387

👤=38€ 👥=52€

Pensión Rúa
- 📞 Calle Lugo 130 – 1º
- ☎ +34 9 8150 0139
- ✉ pensionrua@hotmail.com
- 🏠 www.pensionrua.com
- 📞 42.92905, -8.15539
- ☎ +34 6 9616 2695

👤=38€ 👥=52€

Chapter 7 - Arzúa to Pedrouzo (Arca)

Waypoints Arzúa to Pedrouzo

From	Waypoint	Decimal GPS	Distance	3.9 km/hr	4.6 km/hr	5.3 km/hr
Arzúa	Pregontoño	42.92262 -8.18562	2.3km	0hrs 41mins	0hrs 34mins	0hrs 30mins
Pregontoño	A Peroxa	42.92670 -8.19505	1.0km	0hrs 20mins	0hrs 17mins	0hrs 15mins
A Peroxa	As Quintas	42.92839 -8.21483	1.7km	0hrs 32mins	0hrs 27mins	0hrs 24mins
As Quintas	A Calzada	42.92575 -8.22339	0.8km	0hrs 14mins	0hrs 12mins	0hrs 10mins
A Calzada	A Calle	42.91823 -8.24335	2.1km	0hrs 36mins	0hrs 31mins	0hrs 27mins
A Calle	Salceda	42.92641 -8.28033	3.2km	0hrs 59mins	0hrs 50mins	0hrs 43mins
Salceda	A Brea	42.91886 -8.30530	2.5km	0hrs 46mins	0hrs 39mins	0hrs 34mins
A Brea	Santa Irene	42.91831 -8.33590	2.9km	0hrs 53mins	0hrs 45mins	0hrs 39mins
Santa Irene	A Rua	42.91472 -8.34965	1.4km	0hrs 23mins	0hrs 19mins	0hrs 17mins
A Rua	Pedrouzo	42.90844 -8.36564	2.3km	0hrs 41mins	0hrs 34mins	0hrs 30mins
Arzúa	Pedrouzo	42.90844 -8.36564	20.4km	6hrs 10mins	5hrs 13mins	4hrs 32mins

Arzúa to Pedrouzo Elevation Chart

- Arzúa 388m
- Calzada 388m 5.9km
- Salceda 360m 11.3km
- A Brea 376m 13.8km
- Santa Irene 355m 16.7km
- Pedrouzo 299m 20.4km

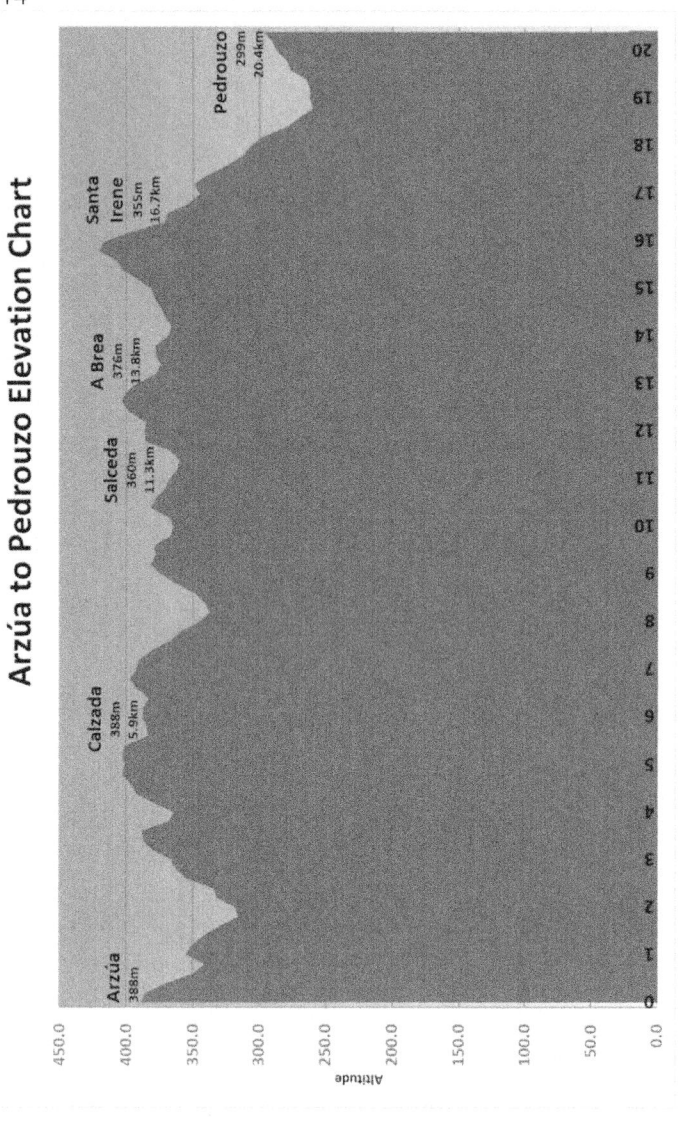

115

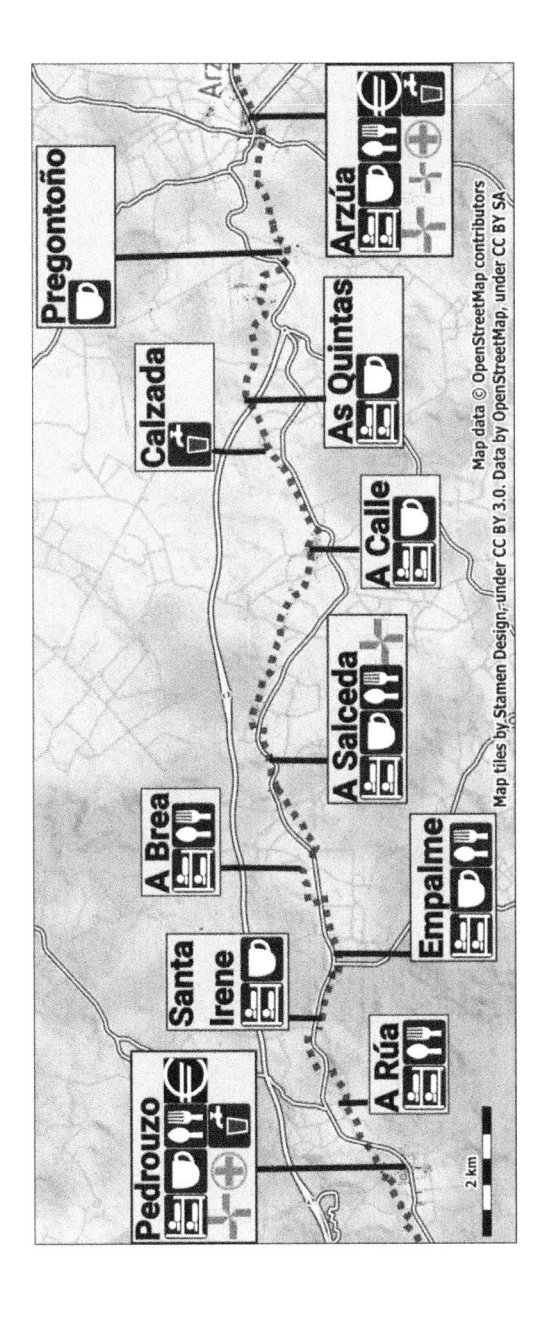

Notes about Today's Stage

Arzúa to Pedrouzo is one of my favourite days of the whole Camino. It is much less demanding than previous days and requires just over six hours of walking. Large parts of today are through wooded areas which makes for some very pleasant walking. Every 4 or 5 kilometres there are places to take a break. The scenery is lush, and many say resembles Galicia's Celtic relative Ireland. In this area it is worth trying the local Arzúa cheese which is rich and creamy because the fat content in the local milk is naturally high. It is best enjoyed with Marmelada which is quince jelly. It is hard to explain why this combination of sweet and savoury works so well, but it must be experienced to appreciate how good it is. While on the subject of food and drink, Galician beer is excellent and is enjoyed all over Northern Spain. In particular, the stronger "toasted" beers often prove to be a Camino favourite.

On the subject of beer, there is a tradition that if you stop in the cafe bar Casa Tia Teresa in the hamlet of Salceda and have a bottle of the Peregrina beer, that you should write your name, your hometown and a wish on the beer bottle. The bar then displays the messages on their Facebook page and keeps the bottles to make a Christmas Tree of good wishes. The tradition originated in the bar Casa Tia Dolores in the hamlet of A Calle where the owners of Casa Tia Teresa were originally based. The new owners of Casa Tia Dolores have also adopted the tradition, so you now have at least two opportunities to enjoy a beer and make a wish.

This day is a day to enjoy and savour. With Santiago, so close at the end of today, you may be tempted to push on further. However, after Pedrouzo there are no albergues until you reach Lavacolla which is an extra 9km further or Monte do Gozo which is an extra 15km! The new albergue at Lavacolla only has limited capacity (only 34 beds) so you need to book ahead. Monte do Gozo is huge and ugly, but it leaves you with only 5km to walk on the final day which makes reaching Santiago in time for the daily pilgrim mass at midday extremely easy. The choice is therefore between stopping at Pedrouzo and having two easy well-balanced last days or going on to Lavacolla or Monte do Gozo and having a tough 30km or 35km penultimate day and extremely easy last day. If you choose to stop at Pedrouzo you will have to leave at around

6 am in order to make it in time for the pilgrim mass. Personally, I recommend Pedrouzo as I really struggle with days above 25km.

Pregontoño

37.6km to Santiago. 1km to A Peroxa. Altitude 334m. Local Facilities= CAFE/BAR. GPS: 42.92262, -8.18562

Notes on Pregontoño

The food and the welcome at the new wooden café/bar in Pregontoño are excellent. The toilets are also excellent, but you need to ask at the bar for them to open the toilets.

Burres (Detour from the Camino)

35.1km to Santiago. Local Facilities= NONE. Burres to Salceda 6.5km.

The albergue in Burres is about an 800m detour from the Camino.

Burres Village Map

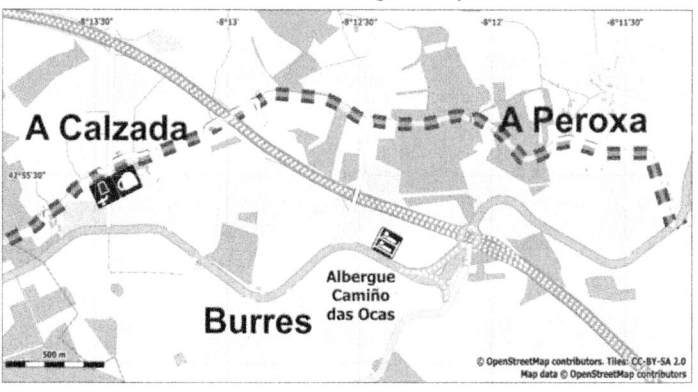

Pilgrim Accommodation Burres

Albergue Camino das Ocas
- N547 Km 68.5 Bebedeiro - Burres
- 42.92163, -8.20688   ☏ +34 6 4840 4780
- contacto@caminodasocas.com
- www.caminodasocas.com

Min Cost= €12, No of Beds = 30, Facilities= KITCHEN, WASHING MACHINE, TUMBLE DRYER
Opening Times: 12:00 till 22:30 March 1 till November 30

A Peroxa
36.6km to Santiago. 1.7km to As Quintas. Altitude 387m. Local Facilities= CAFE/BAR. GPS: 42.9267, -8.19505

As Quintas
34.8km to Santiago. 0.8km to Calzada. Altitude 401m. Local Facilities= CAFE/BAR. GPS: 42.92839, -8.21483

As Quintas Village Map

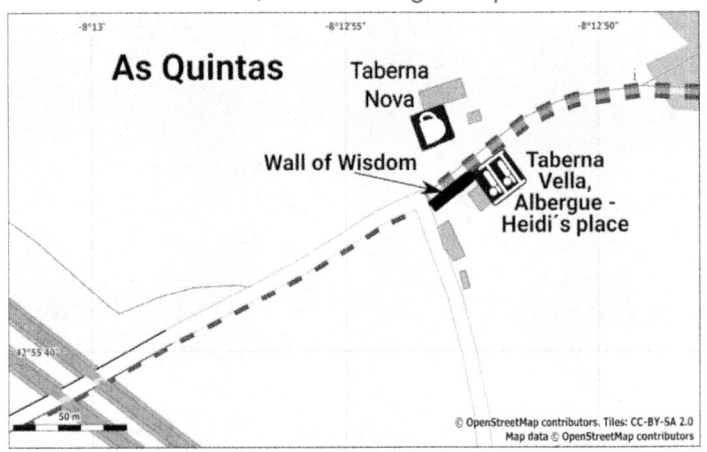

Pilgrim Accommodation As Quintas

Taberna Vella, Albergue - Heidi´s place
- Lugar de Taberna Vella
- ☏ +34 6 8754 3810
- ⌂ taberna-vella.business.site
- 42.92848, -8.21449
- ✉ heidi.tasin@gmail.com

Min Cost= €15, No of Beds = 8, Facilities= KITCHEN, WASHING MACHINE, TUMBLE DRYER, COMMUNAL MEAL
Opening Times: 15:00 till 22:00 April 1 till October 31

Notes on As Quintas

As Quintas is the home of the excellent café/bar Taberna Nova which does excellent tapas including superb bacon sandwiches in brioche bread. The owners from America and England run an upmarket Camino guided tour company which runs guided tours with a support vehicle from Sarria to Santiago as well as the complete Camino from Saint-Jean-Pied-de-Port. Contact details are:

andaspain
☏ +34 6 0828 3238
✉ andaspain@gmail.com
🕸 www.andaspain.com

Calzada

34.0km to Santiago. 2.1km to A Calle. Altitude 388m. Local Facilities= NONE. GPS: 42.92575, -8.22339

A Calle

31.9km to Santiago. 3.2km to Salceda. Altitude 342m. Local Facilities= CAFE/BAR. GPS: 42.91817, -8.24333

A Calle Village Map

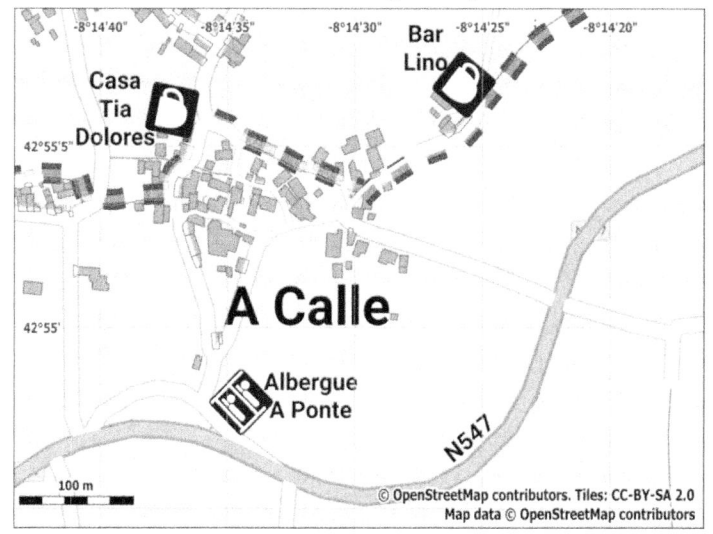

Pilgrim Accommodation A Calle

Albergue A Ponte de Ferreiros
- A Ponte de Ferreiros, 1
- 42.91619, -8.24323
- +34 6 6564 1877
- albergueaponte@gmail.com
- albergueaponte.hol.es

Min Cost= €13, No of Beds = 30, Facilities= KITCHEN, WASHING MACHINE, TUMBLE DRYER, WIFI
Opening Times: 13:00 till 23:00 April 1 till October 31

Private Rooms A Calle

Hotel Rural A Casa do Horreo
- 42.91787, -8.24250
- +34 6 2661 6758
- www.hotelruralcasadohorreo.com

♂=75€ ♂♂=75€

Notes on A Calle

The second cafe/bar in A Calle is Casa Tia Dolores where the tradition of having a beer and writing your name and a wish on the bottle originated. The new owners have carried on the tradition but be warned the new beer they use is over 7% in strength.

Salceda

28.6km to Santiago. 2.5km to A Brea. Altitude 361m. Local Facilities= RESTAURANT, HOTEL OR GUEST HOUSE TYPE ACCOMMODATION, MEDICAL CENTRE. GPS: 42.9263, -8.27842

Salceda Town Map

Notes on Salceda

Salceda despite its tiny size has several albergues and bars, a restaurant, a pension and even a pharmacy. Of note is Casa Tia Teresa. The owners originally ran Café Tia Dolores in A Calle and created the Camino tradition of writing your name and your wish on a beer bottle which they then make into a Christmas tree. Unfortunately, the success of this new tradition led to an increase in rent and a forced move to a new bar in Salceda. I have enjoyed a couple of great afternoons of their hospitality and hence the shout out for their new venture here. Also of note in Salceda is the lovely garden in Meson A Esquipa.

Pilgrim Accommodation Salceda

Albergue La Corona
- Lugar de Salceda, 22
- +34 6 7514 9086
- 42.92654, -8.28009
- +34 9 8107 3382
- alberguelacorona22@gmail.com

Min Cost= €22, No of Beds = 20, Facilities= KITCHEN, WASHING MACHINE, TUMBLE DRYER, WIFI
Opening Times: 12:30 till 20:30 March thru October

Albergue Pousada de Salceda
- N-547 km75
- 42.9221, -8.27552

☎ +34 9 8150 2767
✉ pousadadesalceda@gmail.com
🌐 www.albergueturisticosalceda.com
Min Cost= €13, No of Beds = 8, Facilities= WASHING MACHINE, TUMBLE DRYER, WIFI, SWIMMING POOL, PRIVATE ROOMS AVAILABLE
Opening Times: 12:00 till N/A. Open all year.
🌐 www.booking.com/hotel/es/complejo-turistico-salceda.html

Albergue Alborada
- Lugar de Salceda, Ferreiros o Pino 16
- 42.92627, -8.28052   ☎ +34 6 2015 1209
- ✉ pensionalberguealborada@gmail.com
- 🌐 www.facebook.com/AlbergueAlborada2016

Min Cost= €13, No of Beds = 10, Facilities= WASHING MACHINE, TUMBLE DRYER, WIFI, PRIVATE ROOMS AVAILABLE
Opening Times: 12:30 till 20:00. Open all year.
🌐 www.booking.com/hotel/es/pension-albergue-alborada.html

Private Rooms Salceda

Pensión Casa Tía Teresa
- 42.92560, -8.28212
- ☎ +34 6 2855 8716
- ✉ casatiateresapensionbar@gmail.com
- ♂=35€ ♂♂=40€

Pensión Tasaga
- 42.92655, -8.27937
- ☎ +34 9 8111 3077
- ✉ info@pensiontasaga.com
- 🌐 pensiontasaga.com
- ♂=60€ ♂♂=60€

A Brea

26.1km to Santiago. 2.9km to Santa Irene. Altitude 375m. Local Facilities= CAFE/BAR. GPS: 42.91882, -8.30533

A Brea Village Map

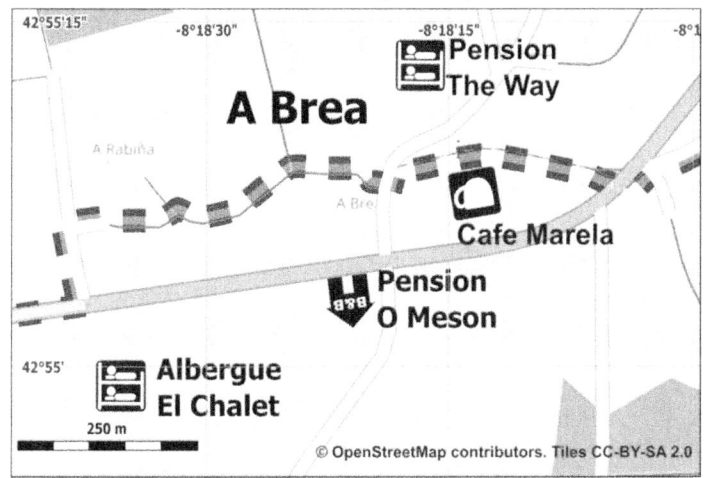

Private Rooms A Brea

Pensión O Meson
- 42.91782, -8.30545
- +34 9 8151 1040
- info@pensionomeson.com
- www.pensionomeson.com
- ♦=30€ ♦♦=42€

Mar de Frisia
- 42.92031, -8.30465
- +34 6 2247 1762
- booking@mardefrisia.es
- www.mardefrisia.es
- ♦=66€ ♦♦=66€

Has nice swimming pool.

Santa Irene

23.2km to Santiago. 1.4km to A Rúa. Altitude 355m. Local Facilities= CAFE/BAR. GPS: 42.91828, -8.33582

Notes on Santa Irene

About 1km before Santa Irene at the road junction at the top of the hill (42.91525, -8.322970) there are two nice restaurant/bars where you can take a break.

Santa Irene Village Map

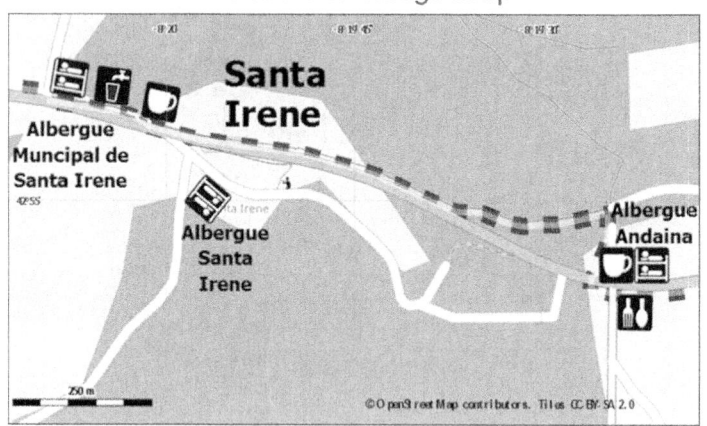

Pilgrim Accommodation Santa Irene

Albergue Xunta
- Santa Irene, s/n - Arca O Pino
- +34 6 6039 6825
- 42.91834, -8.3358
- +34 6 3896 2799

Min Cost= €8, No of Beds = 36, Facilities= KITCHEN, WASHING MACHINE, TUMBLE DRYER
Opening Times: 13:00 till 22:00. Open all year.

Albergue Rural Astrar
- Astrar, 18
- +34 9 8151 1463
- 42.91182, -8.3378
- +34 6 0809 2820

alberguerruralastrar@gmail.com
www.alberguerruralastrar.com
Min Cost= €12, No of Beds = 24, Facilities= KITCHEN, WASHING MACHINE, TUMBLE DRYER, WIFI
Opening Times: 11:00 till 23:00. Open all year.

Albergue Andaina
- Empalme de Santa Irene,11
- 42.91546, -8.32326

☎ +34 9 8150 2925 ☎ +34 6 0973 9404
✉ albergue.andaina@gmail.com
🌐 www.facebook.com/Andaina-965251216896558
Min Cost= €12, No of Beds = 14, Facilities= WASHING MACHINE, TUMBLE DRYER, WIFI
Opening Times: 06:30 till 02:00. Open all year.

Albergue Santa Irene
- Santa Irene, s/n
- 42.91703, -8.33228

☎ +34 9 8151 1000
Min Cost= €13, No of Beds = 15, Facilities= WASHING MACHINE, TUMBLE DRYER, WIFI
Opening Times: 12:00 till 22:00 April 1 till October 31

A Rúa

21.8km to Santiago. 2.3km to O Pedrouzo. Altitude 282m. Local Facilities= CAFE/BAR, RESTAURANT, HOTEL OR GUEST HOUSE TYPE ACCOMMODATION. GPS: 42.91469, -8.3501

A Rúa Village Map

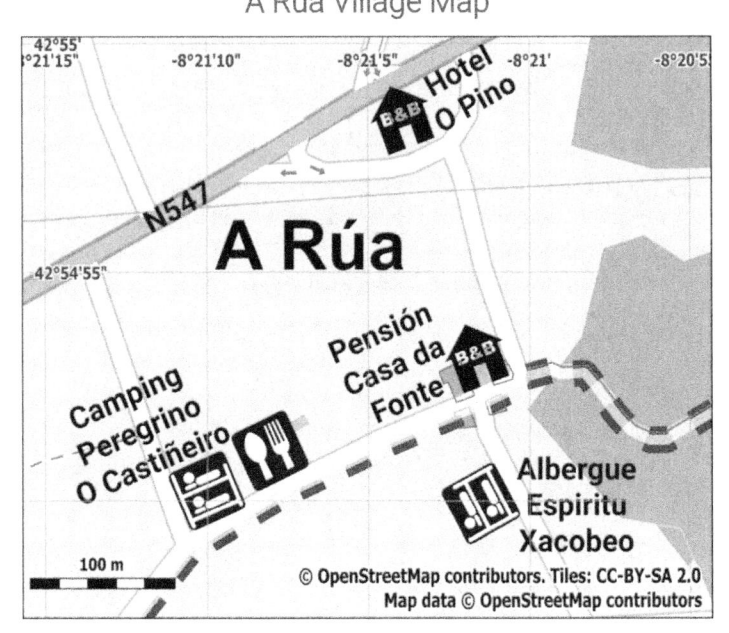

Pilgrim Accommodation A Rúa

Albergue Espíritu Xacobeo
- A Rúa nº 49-50
- 42.91402, -8.35021
- ☏ +34 6 2063 5284
- albergue@espirituxacobeo.com
- www.espirituxacobeo.com

Min Cost= €12, No of Beds = 46, Facilities= KITCHEN, WASHING MACHINE, TUMBLE DRYER, WIFI
Opening Times: 12:00 till 23:00 April 1 till October 31
www.booking.com/hotel/es/albergue-espiritu-xacobeo-o-pedrouzo.html

Camping Peregrino O Castiñeiro
- A Rúa S/N
- 42.91373, -8.35284
- ☏ +34 6 6245 6093
- info@campingperegrino.es
- www.campingperegrino.es

Min Cost= €12, No of Beds = 112, Facilities= WASHING MACHINE, TUMBLE DRYER, WIFI, SWIMMING POOL

Opening Times: 12:00 till 22:00 April 1 till October 31
🏛 www.booking.com/hotel/es/camping-peregrino-o-castineiro.html

Private Rooms A Rúa

Hotel O'Pino
📞 42.91612, -8.35086
☎ +34 9 8151 1148   ☎ +34 9 8151 1035
✉ info@hotelopino.com
🏛 www.hotelopino.com
♂=45€ ♂♂=60€
Pleasant. Good reports on menu del día, 12€. Clean. Used by groups. Tends to get crowded.

Casa do Acivro
📞 42.91403, -8.35205
☎ +34 9 8151 1316   ☎ +34 6 0910 5948
✉ cacivro@hotmail.es
🏛 oacivro.com
♂=75€ ♂♂=75€
Outdoor swimming pool & A/C.

Pedrouzo (Arca)

19.6km to Santiago. 2.6km to Amenal. Altitude 262m. Local Facilities= CAFE/BAR, RESTAURANT, ATM, HOTEL OR GUEST HOUSE TYPE ACCOMMODATION, PHARMACY, MEDICAL CENTRE, GROCERY STORE. GPS: 42.91205, -8.357725

Notes on Pedrouzo (Arca)

Pedrouzo is also known as Arca. It is a relatively modern town though recent excavations have revealed a pilgrim cemetery which is thought to have been attached to the Hospital de Santa Eulalia de Arca of which nothing remains. You have to detour off the Camino to enter the main street in Pedrouzo which has several bars/cafes and restaurants to service the needs of the pilgrims. As this is the last major stopping point before Santiago, accommodation is often fully booked so it is advisable to book in advance as the next major albergue is another 15 km away.

There are several reasonable restaurants in Pedrouzo but of note is "Taste the Way" which is on the high street and also offers a really good take-out service. The restaurant "O Pedrouzo" on Rúa Concello offers only two options either veal steak or veal chop but both options are magnificent. The meat is partially cooked and cut into strips which you then finish cooking to your choice on a hot stone on the table. All in all, a truly memorable experience.

Pedrouzo (Arca) Town Map

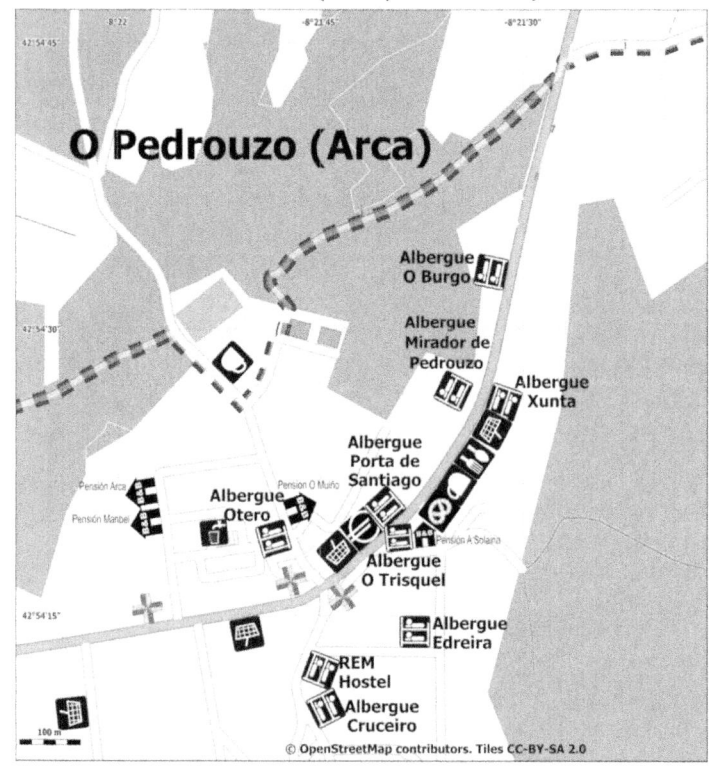

Pilgrim Accommodation Pedrouzo

Albergue Xunta de Arca do Pino
- O Pedrouzo - Arca, s/n O Pino
- 42.90703, -8.35883
- +34 6 4988 0954
- +34 6 5081 2040

Min Cost= €8, No of Beds = 126, Facilities= KITCHEN, WASHING MACHINE, TUMBLE DRYER, WIFI

Opening Times: 13:00 till 22:00. Open all year.

Albergue Cruceiro de Pedrouzo
- Avenida de la Iglesia 7
- 42.90303, -8.36297
- +34 9 8151 1371
- +34 6 2951 8204
- reservas@alberguecruceirodepedrouzo.com
- www.alberguecruceirodepedrouzo.com

Min Cost= €12, No of Beds = 94, Facilities= KITCHEN, WASHING MACHINE, TUMBLE DRYER, WIFI
Opening Times: 12:00 till 23:00 March 1 till November 30

Albergue Edreira
- Rúa da Fonte, 19
- 42.90367, -8.36056
- +34 6 6023 4995
- info@albergue-edreira.com
- www.albergue-edreira.com

Min Cost= €12, No of Beds = 52, Facilities= KITCHEN, WASHING MACHINE, WIFI
Opening Times: 12:00 till 23:00 March 1 till October 31

Albergue O Trisquel
- Rúa Picón, 1
- 42.90501, -8.3612
- +34 6 1664 4740
- informatrisquel@gmail.com
- www.facebook.com/o.trisquel.albergue

Min Cost= €12, No of Beds = 68, Facilities= KITCHEN, WASHING MACHINE, WIFI
Opening Times: 11:00 till 23:00 March 1 till October 31
- www.booking.com/hotel/es/albergue-o-trisquel.html

Hostel Rem
- Avenida da Igrexa 7
- 42.90319, -8.36299
- +34 9 8151 0407
- +34 7 2244 8211
- reservas@alberguerem.com
- www.alberguerem.com

Min Cost= €12, No of Beds = 40, Facilities= WASHING MACHINE, TUMBLE DRYER, WIFI
Opening Times: 11:00 till 23:00 April 1 till October 31

Albergue Otero
- Rúa Forcarey, 2
- 42.90506, -8.36336
- +34 6 7166 3374
- info@albergueotero.com
- www.albergueotero.com

Min Cost= €12, No of Beds = 36, Facilities= KITCHEN, WASHING MACHINE, TUMBLE DRYER, WIFI
Opening Times: 11:00 till 23:00 April 1 till November 30

Albergue Turistico O Burgo

Avenida de Lugo, 47 — 42.90905, -8.35874
+34 6 3040 4138 — +34 9 8151 1406
info@albergueoburgo.es — www.albergueoburgo.es
Min Cost= €10, No of Beds = 24, Facilities= WASHING MACHINE, TUMBLE DRYER, PRIVATE ROOMS AVAILABLE
Opening Times: 12:00 till 23:00 April 1 till November 30

Albergue Mirador de Pedrouzo

Avenida de Lugo S / N — 42.90701, -8.3599
+34 6 8687 1215
info@miradordepedrouzo.com
www.alberguemiradordepedrouzo.com
Min Cost= €15, No of Beds = 50, Facilities= KITCHEN, WASHING MACHINE, TUMBLE DRYER, WIFI, PRIVATE ROOMS AVAILABLE
Opening Times: 12:00 till 23:00. Open all year.
www.booking.com/hotel/es/mirador-de-pedrouzo.html

Private Rooms Pedrouzo

Casa Santaia

Avenida da Igrexa, 10 — 42.90138, -8.36280
+34 6 7671 3823
santaiadacalma@gmail.com
casasantaia.com
1 person=55€ 2 persons=65€

Pensión LO

42.90643, -8.36441
+34 6 0898 9100
pensionlo.com
1 person=53€ 2 persons=63€
On the Camino on the way out of town. Laundry service available.

Pensión Una Estrella Dorada

42.90514, -8.36137
+34 6 3001 8363
pension-una-estrella-dorada.business.site
1 person=40€ 2 persons=55€

Pensión 9 de Abril
- Avenida Santiago, 7
- 42.90424, -8.36332
- ☏ +34 6 0676 4762
- ✉ infopension9deabril@gmail.com
- 🌐 www.pension9deabril.com
- 👤=40€ 👥=50€

Pensión Arca
- Rúa Os Mollados, 25
- 42.90611, -8.36579
- ☏ +34 6 5788 8594
- ☏ +34 9 8151 1437
- 🌐 www.pensionarca.com
- 👤=35€ 👥=50€

Pensión A Solaina
- Rúa do Picón
- 42.90509, -8.36036
- ☏ +34 6 3353 0918
- ✉ pensionasolaina@hotmail.com
- 🌐 www.pensionasolaina.com
- 👤=45€ 👥=45€

Pensión Maribel
- Rúa Os Mollados, 23
- 42.90590, -8.36583
- ☏ +34 9 8151 1404
- ☏ +34 6 0945 9966
- ✉ info@pensionmaribel.com
- 🌐 www.pensionmaribel.com
- 👤=38€ 👥=45€

Pensión O Pedrouzo
- Avenida Santiago, 13
- 42.90413, -8.36428
- ☏ +34 6 7166 3375
- ☏ +34 9 8151 0483
- ✉ info@pensionpedrouzo.com
- 🌐 www.pensionpedrouzo.com
- 👤=38€ 👥=45€

Pensión Platas
- Avenida de Lugo, 26
- 42.90674, -8.35937
- ☏ +34 9 8151 1378
- 🌐 www.pensionplatas.es
- 👤=50€ 👥=70€

I love the messages of encouragement that you often find scrawled by previous pilgrims. This one translates as "Let nothing worry you".

Chapter 8 - Pedrouzo to Santiago de Compostela

Waypoints Pedrouzo to Santiago de Compostela

From	Waypoint	Decimal GPS	Distance	3.9 km/hr	4.6 km/hr	5.3 km/hr
Pedrouzo	Amenal	42.90519 -8.39158	2.6km	0hrs 46mins	0hrs 39mins	0hrs 34mins
Amenal	San Paio	42.90870 -8.42616	4.2km	1hrs 20mins	1hrs 7mins	0hrs 58mins
San Paio	Lavacolla	42.89746 -8.44662	2.7km	0hrs 48mins	0hrs 41mins	0hrs 35mins
Lavacolla	Vilamaior	42.89215 -8.44982	0.8km	0hrs 16mins	0hrs 14mins	0hrs 12mins
Vilamaior	San Marcos	42.89130 -8.48937	3.7km	1hrs 6mins	0hrs 56mins	0hrs 49mins
San Marcos	Monte del Gozo	42.88821 -8.49867	0.9km	0hrs 16mins	0hrs 13mins	0hrs 11mins
Monte del Gozo	Santiago Puerta del Camino	42.88185 -8.54020	4.0km	1hrs 11mins	1hrs 0mins	0hrs 52mins
Santiago Puerta del Camino	Santiago Cathedral	42.88069 -8.54537	0.5km	0hrs 9mins	0hrs 8mins	0hrs 7mins
Pedrouzo	Santiago Cathedral	42.88069 -8.54537	19.6km	5hrs 56mins	5hrs 2mins	4hrs 22mins

Pedrouzo to Santiago de Compostela Elevation Chart

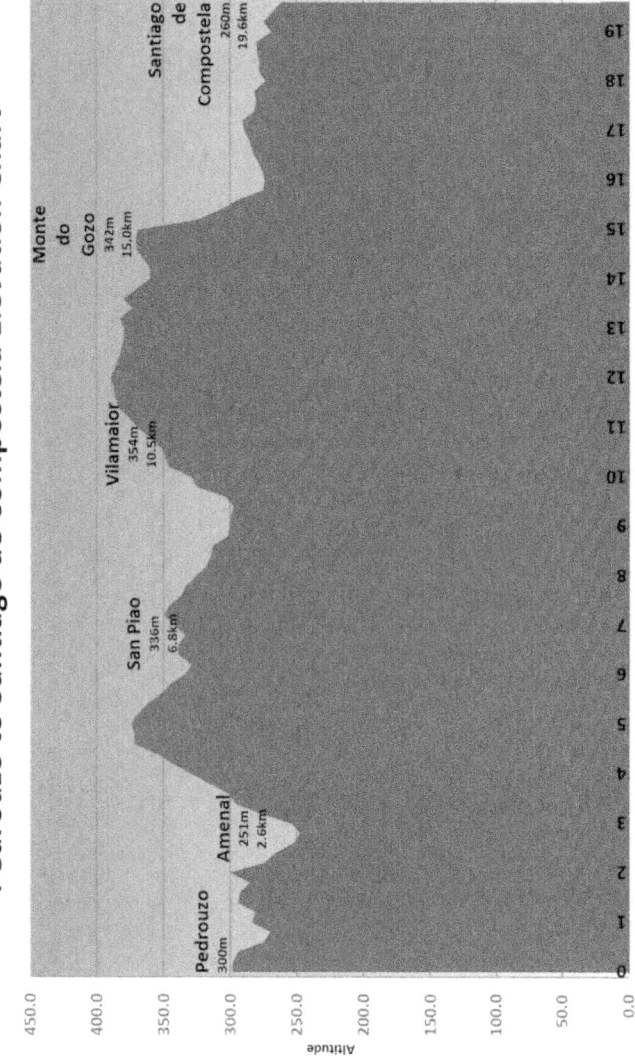

- Pedrouzo 300m
- Amenal 251m 2.6km
- San Piao 336m 6.8km
- Vilamaior 354m 10.5km
- Monte do Gozo 342m 15.0km
- Santiago de Compostela 260m 19.6km

135

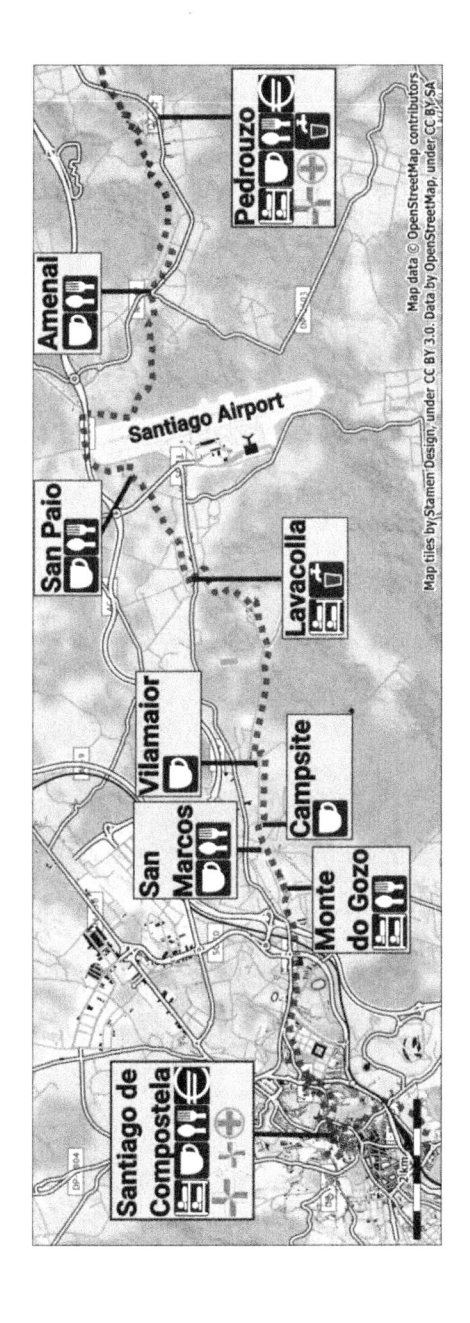

Notes about Today's Stage

The first part of today's walk is through wooded paths. The trees are particularly tall and there are many Eucalyptus trees among them which makes for very aromatic and pleasant walking. However, it is also particularly dark especially early in the morning so make sure you have a torch with you. The path is littered with mojones (the stone way markers) and is easy to follow even in the dark, with one exception. This exception is at the point where you come out of the woods for the second time, where the nearest mojón is about 100m down on the left and is not easily visible.

There is just one other albergue (in Lavacolla) on this leg apart from the huge albergue at Monte do Gozo but there are a few cafe/bars along the way where you can grab some breakfast or just take a break. The atmosphere is often buzzing with groups singing along the final leg of their pilgrimage. By this stage most of the other Caminos have joined so it is a busy stage and better for celebratory walking rather than reflective walking you may have enjoyed earlier in the week. On the way up to Monte do Gozo you will pass the local TV stations. On arriving at Monte de Gozo, you will see a large monument which commemorates the visit of Pope John Paul 2 in 1989 and St Francis of Assisi's pilgrimage in 1214. The Monte do Gozo grounds are large and not of great architectural merit except for the viewing point (mirador). This mirador consists of two very large statues of medieval pilgrims catching their first excited view of the cathedral at Santiago. It is a bit of a detour to visit the viewing point so most pilgrims skip this and head straight for Santiago. You are now on the outskirts of the city and like most city walking, walking on concrete is tiring on the feet. Although Santiago appears close, it will take you another 80 minutes before you arrive at your final destination, the cathedral.

Amenal

17.0km to Santiago. 4.2km to San Paio. Altitude 251m. Local Facilities=RESTAURANT, HOTEL OR GUEST HOUSE TYPE ACCOMMODATION. GPS: 42.90530, -8.39157

Notes on Amenal

There is a new café/bar at Amenal about 10 metres before the hotel. In my experience this was small and overwhelmed with little choice for breakfast. My preference is therefore to stop at the café/bar of the small hotel at Amenal. This opens at 7am during the winter and 6am during the summer months and if you are leaving Pedrouzo before 6am to catch the pilgrim's mass this may be your first opportunity for breakfast. The Camino passes by the side of the hotel and after about 2km you will come across the perimeter of the airport. You will then walk around the end of the airport (including underneath the end of the runway) around to the other side.

Private Rooms Amenal

Hotel Amenal
- 42.90570, -8.39439
- +34 9 8151 0431
- reservas@hotelamenal.com
- www.hotelamenal.com
- ♂=65€ ♂♂=65€

Pensión Kilómetro 15
- 42.90588, -8.39335
- +34 9 8181 4300
- barkilometro15.negocio.site
- ♂=43€ ♂♂=53€

San Paio

12.7km to Santiago. 2.7km to Lavacolla. Altitude 334m. Local Facilities= RESTAURANT. GPS: 42.90891, -8.42613

Notes on San Paio

If you miss the right turn to San Paio you can end up at the airport terminal. If you do end up at the airport terminal, you just follow the signposts for Santiago and you eventually end up back on the Camino. By the time, you have reached San Paio most, but not all, of the Caminos have come together so numbers will have significantly increased. The first cafe/bar in San Paio (called A Casa de Porta de Santiago) if its open, will insist you buy something if you want to use the toilets as there is often a big demand for toilets at this stop. However, opposite the rear of the church is a second lovely bar with a shaded courtyard. The church dates from 1840 and is built on the site of a 12th century monastery. Often there are stalls setup outside selling all kinds of pilgrim mementoes and jewellery. The village and the church are dedicated to San Paio (also known as San Payo or San Pelayo) who was a young boy from Tui/Tuy in Galicia who was martyred in 925 by being pulled apart by iron tongs for refusing to renounce his Christian faith.

Private Rooms San Paio

Last 12K Premium Guest House
- 42.90900, -8.42652
- ☏ +34 6 1990 4743
- ♂=65€ ♂♂=65€

Lovely courtyard bar.

Lavacolla

10.0km to Santiago. 0.8km to Vilamaior. Altitude 298m. Local Facilities=HOTEL OR GUEST HOUSE TYPE ACCOMMODATION. GPS: 42.89979, -8.44662

Pilgrim Accommodation Lavacolla

Albergue Lavacolla
- Lavacolla 35
- ☏ +34 9 8189 7274
- 42.89948, -8.44387
- ☏ +34 6 5363 0300
- ✉ reservas@alberguelavacolla.com
- 🌐 www.alberguelavacolla.com

Min Cost= €12, No of Beds = 34, Facilities= KITCHEN, WIFI
Opening Times: 13:30 till 21:00 April 1 till November 30

Private Rooms Lavacolla

Hotel Ruta Jacobea
- 42.89972, -8.44106
- ☏ +34 9 8188 8211
- ✉ comercial@rjacobea.com
- 🌐 rjacobea.com
- ♂=89€ ♂♂=89€

Hostal A Concha

- 42.89983, -8.44723
- +34 9 8188 8390
- ♦=25€ ♦♦=30€

Pensión Xacobeo Lavacolla
- 42.90093, -8.44451
- +34 6 0836 3658
- ♦=60€ ♦♦=60€

Pensión Dorotea
- 42.90007, -8.44760
- +34 6 1942 4969
- ♦=50€ ♦♦=50€

Notes on Lavacolla

Lavacolla is described in the Codex Calixtinus as the place where pilgrims would take off all their clothes and wash themselves in the river. This was done out of respect for and in preparation for meeting Saint James. Even after a few days it is possible to appreciate that maintaining personal hygiene standards whilst living out of a backpack and walking 23km per day is challenging. However, I am not sure this is a tradition I would like to see come back into fashion as the river in question is an exceedingly small stream these days, completely unsuitable for bathing.

Vilamaior

9.2km to Santiago. 3.7km to San Marcos. Altitude 351m. Local Facilities=RESTAURANT. GPS: 42.89215, -8.44983

San Marcos

5.5km to Santiago. 0.9km to Monte do Gozo. Altitude 361m. Local Facilities= CAFE/BAR, RESTAURANT, HOTEL OR GUEST HOUSE TYPE ACCOMMODATION. GPS: 42.89120, -8.48944

Notes on San Marcos

The camping site cafe/bar on the corner at the very start of San Marcos is the traditional last rest stop before Santiago itself but in 2018 a brand-new restaurant / bar called A Calzada has opened 1.2km further down road in San Marcos itself.

Monte do Gozo

4.6km to Santiago. 4.6km to Santiago de Compostela. Altitude 339m. Local Facilities= CAFE/BAR, RESTAURANT. GPS: 42.88741, -8.49817

Notes on Monte do Gozo

Monte de Gozo means mount of joy and refers to the joy that most pilgrims feel at reaching the top of this last hill before Santiago. The atmosphere is really buzzing by this point. Tradition holds that even those who have made the pilgrimage on horseback dismount and walk the last 4 or 5 km in by foot. It is not a tradition that has yet been adopted by the bicigrinos but I think it would make a nice tradition if all pilgrims could walk in together as one.

If you want to enjoy the traditional view that medieval pilgrims enjoyed of Santiago, it is about a 10-minute detour to the mirador with the two huge pilgrim statues. As the route from the mirador back on to the Camino is not marked I would suggest after visiting the mirador to head back to the main (JP II/Saint Francis) monument and re-join the Camino there.

From here on in its downhill pretty much all the way and after many days of uphill and downhill that is a joy in itself. From here also you are on the outskirts of the city and as any seasoned walker will tell you city walking is the most draining as it is literally hard on your feet. As you get closer there are progressively more bars and cafes where you can give your poor feet 5 minutes rest and enjoy a soft drink before the final push into the centre of Praza do Obradoiro where your pilgrimage officially ends.

Please note that for security reasons you will not be allowed into the cathedral with a full backpack although you may be allowed in with a small daypack which will be searched. However, if you have a backpack there is no problem as next to the entrance to the cathedral on the corner is a facility where for a small fee they will store your backpack for several hours giving you time to visit the cathedral, go to the Pilgrim's Office to get your Compostela and have some lunch before you head off to find your accommodation.

Monte do Gozo Village Map

Pilgrim Accommodation Monte do Gozo

Albergue Xunta del Monte do Gozo
- Rúa do Gozo, 1
- 42.88722, -8.49989
- ☎ +34 9 8155 8942
- ☎ +34 6 3896 2797

Min Cost= €8, No of Beds = 400, Facilities= WASHING MACHINE, TUMBLE DRYER, BICYCLE STORAGE
Opening Times: 13:00 till 22:00. Open all year.

John Paul II (Polish Albergue)
- Rúa das Estrelas, 80
- 42.88694, -8.49382
- ☎ +34 9 8159 7222
- ceperegrinacion@alfaexpress.net

Min Cost= €Don, No of Beds = 40, Facilities= KITCHEN, WASHING MACHINE, COMMUNAL MEAL, PRIVATE ROOMS AVAILABLE
Opening Times: 13:00 till 22:00. Open all year.

Albergue Monte do Gozo
- Rúa do Gozo, 18
- 42.8863, -8.50123
- ☎ +34 8 8125 5386
- info@montedogozo.com
- www.montedogozo.com

Min Cost= €23, No of Beds = 80, Facilities= WASHING MACHINE, TUMBLE DRYER, WIFI, SWIMMING POOL, COMMUNAL MEAL, PRIVATE ROOMS AVAILABLE

Opening Times: 15:00 till 22:00. Open all year.

🕌 www.booking.com/hotel/es/benvido-monte-do-gozo.html

Chapter 9 - Santiago de Compostela

0km to Santiago. Altitude 261m. Local Facilities= CAFE/BAR, RESTAURANT, ATM, HOTEL OR GUEST HOUSE TYPE ACCOMMODATION, PHARMACY, MEDICAL CENTRE, GROCERY STORE. GPS: 42.88059, -8.545186

Map of Greater Santiago

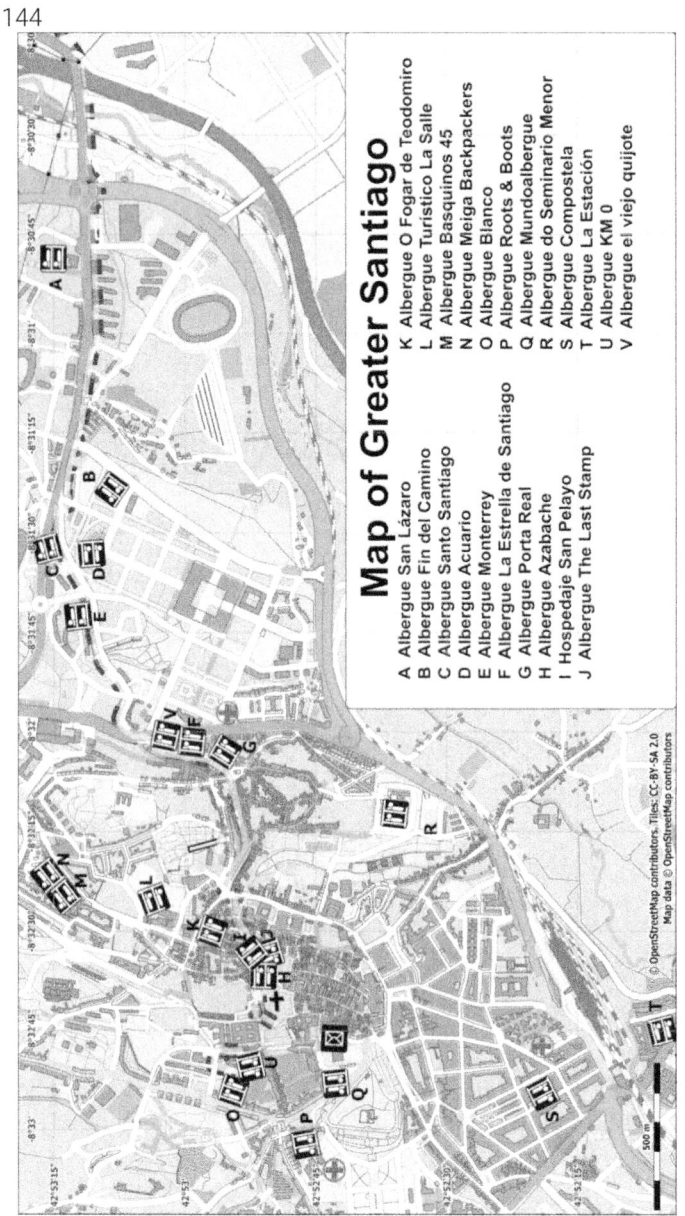

- A Albergue San Lázaro
- B Albergue Fin del Camino
- C Albergue Santo Santiago
- D Albergue Acuario
- E Albergue Monterrey
- F Albergue La Estrella de Santiago
- G Albergue Porta Real
- H Albergue Azabache
- I Hospedaje San Pelayo
- J Albergue The Last Stamp
- K Albergue O Fogar de Teodomiro
- L Albergue Turistico La Salle
- M Albergue Basquiños 45
- N Albergue Meiga Backpackers
- O Albergue Blanco
- P Albergue Roots & Boots
- Q Albergue Mundoalbergue
- R Albergue do Seminario Menor
- S Albergue Compostela
- T Albergue La Estación
- U Albergue KM 0
- V Albergue el viejo quijote

145

Map of Central Santiago

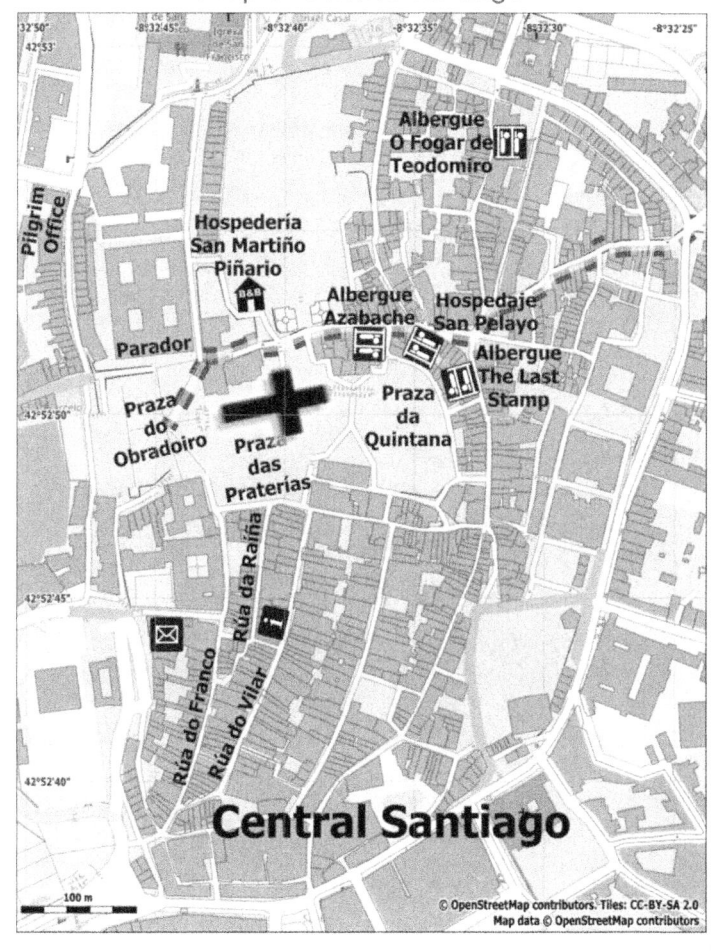

Pilgrim Accommodation Santiago de Compostela

Albergue Fin del Camino
- Rúa de Moscova
- 42.88528, -8.52333
- +34 9 8158 7324
- albergue@fundacionperegrinacionasantiago.com
- www.alberguefindelcamino.com

Min Cost= €10, No of Beds = 150, Facilities= KITCHEN, WASHING MACHINE, TUMBLE DRYER, WIFI, PRIVATE ROOMS AVAILABLE
Opening Times: 11:30 till 00:00 May 1 till September 30

Albergue Xunta San Lázaro
- Rúa San Lázaro
- 42.887386, -8.51322
- +34 9 8157 1488
- +34 6 2692 5625

Min Cost= €8, No of Beds = 80, Facilities= KITCHEN, WASHING MACHINE, TUMBLE DRYER,
Opening Times: 09:00 till 22:00. Open all year.
TEMPORARILY CLOSED since 27/09/2021.

Albergue Santo Santiago
- Rúa do Valiño, 3
- 42.88711, -8.52592
- +34 6 5740 2403
- elsantosantiago@gmail.com

Min Cost= €12, No of Beds = 40, Facilities= WASHING MACHINE, TUMBLE DRYER, WIFI
Opening Times: 09:00 till N/A. Open all year.
- www.booking.com/hotel/es/albergue-santo-santiago.html

Albergue La Credencial
- Fonte dos Concheiros, 13 Bajo
- 42.88525, -8.53222
- +34 9 8106 8083
- +34 6 3996 6704
- reservas@lacredencial.es
- www.lacredencial.es

Min Cost= €14, No of Beds = 36, Facilities= KITCHEN, WASHING MACHINE, TUMBLE DRYER, WIFI
Opening Times: 11:00 till 22:00 March 1 till November 30
- www.booking.com/hotel/es/albergue-turistico-la-credencial.html

Albergue La Estrella de Santiago
- Rúa Concheiros, 36-38
- 42.88321, -8.53415
- +34 6 1788 2529
- +34 8 8197 3926

info@laestrelladesantiago.es
www.laestrelladesantiago.es
Min Cost= €16, No of Beds = 24, Facilities= KITCHEN, WASHING MACHINE, WIFI
Opening Times: 09:00 till 22:00. Open all year.

Albergue Porta Real
- Rúa dos Concheiros, 10
- 42.88222, -8.53462
- +34 6 3361 0114
- reservas@albergueportareal.es
- albergueportareal.es

Min Cost= €16, No of Beds = 20, Facilities= WASHING MACHINE, TUMBLE DRYER, WIFI
Opening Times: No check-in restrictions. Open all year.
www.booking.com/hotel/es/albergue-porta-real.html

Albergue Seminario Menor de Belvis
- Avenida Quiroga Palacios
- 42.877206, -8.537332
- +34 8 8103 1768
- +34 9 8156 8521
- santiago@alberguesdelcamino.com
- www.alberguesdelcamino.com

Min Cost= €15, No of Beds = 177, Facilities= KITCHEN, WASHING MACHINE, TUMBLE DRYER, WIFI PRIVATE ROOMS AVAILABLE
Opening Times: 13:30 till 00:00 March 1 till October 31

Albergue Blanco
- Rúa das Galeras, 30
- 42.8819, -8.54888
- +34 8 8197 6850
- +34 6 9959 1238
- prblanco@prblanco.com
- www.prblanco.com

Min Cost= €20, No of Beds = 20, Facilities= KITCHEN, WASHING MACHINE, TUMBLE DRYER, WIFI PRIVATE ROOMS AVAILABLE
Opening Times: 12:00 till N/A. Open all year.
www.booking.com/hotel/es/blanco-albergue.html

Albergue Meiga Backpackers
- Rúa Baquiños, 67
- 42.88742, -8.53885
- +34 9 8157 0846
- info_meiga@yahoo.es
- www.meiga-backpackers.es

Min Cost= €17, No of Beds = 18, Facilities= WASHING MACHINE, TUMBLE DRYER, WIFI
Opening Times: 10:00 till 22:00 January 7 till December 23

Albergue La Estacion
- Rúa Xoana Nogueira, 14
- +34 9 8159 4624
- 42.86856, -8.5458
- +34 6 3922 8617
- info@alberguelaestacion.com
- www.alberguelaestacion.com

Min Cost= €15, No of Beds = 24, Facilities= KITCHEN, WASHING MACHINE, TUMBLE DRYER, WIFI PRIVATE ROOMS AVAILABLE
Opening Times: 13:00 till 00:00 Holy Week till September 30

Albergue Monterrey
- Rúa das Fontiñas, 65, Bajo
- +34 8 8112 5093
- 42.88629, -8.52839
- +34 6 5548 4299
- alberguemonterrey@gmail.com
- alberguemonterrey.es

Min Cost= €14, No of Beds = 36, Facilities= KITCHEN, WASHING MACHINE, TUMBLE DRYER, WIFI
Opening Times: 12:00 till 22:00. Open all year.
- www.booking.com/hotel/es/albergue-monterrey.html

Albergue The last Stamp
- Rúa Preguntorio, 10
- +34 9 8156 3525
- 42.88089, -8.54246
- reservas@thelaststamp.es
- www.thelaststamp.es

Min Cost= €20, No of Beds = 62, Facilities= KITCHEN, WASHING MACHINE, TUMBLE DRYER, WIFI PRIVATE ROOMS AVAILABLE
Opening Times: 14:00 till N/A January 16 till December 14
- www.booking.com/hotel/es/the-last-stamp.html

Albergue/Hotel LoopINN
- Tras Santa Clara
- +34 6 8215 8011
- 42.88482, -8.54043
- +34 9 8158 5667
- info@loopinnhostels.com
- loopinnhostels.com/santiago/

Min Cost= €21, No of Beds = 20, Facilities= KITCHEN, WASHING MACHINE, TUMBLE DRYER, WIFI PRIVATE ROOMS AVAILABLE
Opening Times: No check-in restrictions. Open all year.
- www.booking.com/hotel/es/hostal-la-salle.html

Albergue Mundoalbergue
- Calle San Clemente, 26
- +34 9 8158 8625
- 42.87863, -8.54754
- +34 6 9644 8737
- info@mundoalbergue.es
- www.mundoalbergue.es

Min Cost= €18, No of Beds = 34, Facilities= KITCHEN, WASHING MACHINE, TUMBLE DRYER, WIFI
Opening Times: 12:00 till N/A. Open all year.

Albergue Azabache
- Rúa Acibechería 15
- 42.88122, -8.54354
- +34 9 8107 1254
- +34 6 9210 5603
- azabachehostel@yahoo.es
- albergueazabache.com

Min Cost= €18, No of Beds = 20, Facilities= KITCHEN, WASHING MACHINE, TUMBLE DRYER,
Opening Times: 12:00 till 22:00. Open all year.

Albergue Santiago KM.0
- Rúa das Carretas, 11
- 42.88126, -8.54677
- +34 8 8197 4992
- info@santiagokm0.es
- santiagokm0.es

Min Cost= €20, No of Beds = 41, Facilities= KITCHEN, WASHING MACHINE, TUMBLE DRYER, WIFI
Opening Times: 13:00 till N/A February 28 till December 22
- www.booking.com/hotel/es/santiago-km0.html

Albergue SIXTOS no Caminho
- Rúa da Fonte dos Concheiros, 2A (baixos)
- 42.88501, -8.53318
- +34 8 8102 4195
- +34 6 9007 7832
- albergue@sixtosnocaminho.com
- alberguesixtos.com

Min Cost= €20, No of Beds = 40, Facilities= KITCHEN, WASHING MACHINE, TUMBLE DRYER, WIFI, PRIVATE ROOMS AVAILABLE
Opening Times: 11:00 till 22:30 February 1 till November 30
- www.booking.com/hotel/es/albergue-sixtos-no-caminho-santiago-de-compostela.html

Albergue SCQ
- Rúa da Fonte dos Concheiros, 2C
- 42.88529, -8.53279
- +34 6 2203 7300
- alberguescq@gmail.com

Min Cost= €16, No of Beds = 24, Facilities= KITCHEN, WASHING MACHINE, TUMBLE DRYER, WIFI
Opening Times: 09:30 till 22:00. Open all year.
- www.booking.com/hotel/es/albergue-scq.html

Albergue Santos
- Rúa dos Concheiros, 48
- 42.88361, -8.53405
- +34 8 8116 9386
- as.alberguesantos@gmail.com

Min Cost= €18, No of Beds = 22, Facilities= KITCHEN, WASHING MACHINE, TUMBLE DRYER, WIFI
Opening Times: 10:30 till 21:00. Open March thru November.

Albergue Alda O Fogar de Teodomiro
- Praciña da Algalia de Arriba, 3
- 42.88257, -8.54212
- +34 8 8109 2981
- fogarteodomiro@aldahotels.com
- aldahotels.es/alojamientos/albergue-alda-o-fogar-de-teodomiro/

Min Cost= €14, No of Beds = 24, Facilities= KITCHEN, WASHING MACHINE, TUMBLE DRYER, WIFI
Opening Times: 15:00 till 21:00. Open all year.
- www.booking.com/hotel/es/o-fogar-de-teodomiro.html

Albergue A Fonte de Compostela
- Rúa Estocolmo, 172
- 42.88670, -8.52623
- +34 6 0401 9115
- +34 8 8129 0468
- compostela@alberguesafonte.com
- alberguesafonte.com

Min Cost= €14, No of Beds = 30, Facilities= KITCHEN, WASHING MACHINE, TUMBLE DRYER, WIFI
Opening Times: 16:30 till 20:00. Open all year.
- www.booking.com/hotel/es/a-fonte-de-compostela.html

Albergue Dream in Santiago
- Rúa San Lázaro, 81
- 42.88650, -8.51607
- +34 9 8194 3208
- reservas@dreaminsantiago.com
- dreaminsantiago.com

Min Cost= €18, No of Beds = 60, Facilities= KITCHEN, WASHING MACHINE, TUMBLE DRYER, WIFI
Opening Times: 15:30 till 20:00. March thru October.
- www.booking.com/hotel/es/dream-in-santiago.html

Albergue Linares
- Rúa da Algalia de Abaixo, 34
- 42.88290, -8.54163
- +34 9 8194 3253
- linares@grupogescaho.com

🏠 www.linaresroomssantiago.com
Min Cost= €16, No of Beds = 14, Facilities= WASHING MACHINE, TUMBLE DRYER, WIFI
Opening Times: 13:00 till 17:00. Open all year.
🏠 www.booking.com/hotel/es/albergue-linares.html

Private Rooms in Santiago de Compostela

Hostal dos Reis Católicos - Parador
- Praza do Obradoiro, 1
- 42.88095, -8.54585
- ☎ +34 981 582 200
- ✉ santiago@parador.es
- 🏠 www.parador.es/es/paradores/parador-de-santiago-de-compostela
- ♂=137€ ♂♂=165€

Hospedería San Martín Pinario
- Plaza de la Inmaculada,3
- 42.88132, -8.54467
- ☎ +34 981 560 282
- ✉ info@sanmartinpinario.eu
- 🏠 www.hsanmartinpinario.com
- ♂=50€ ♂♂=57€ (There are also un-refurbished rooms on the top floor for pilgrims only, please contact the Hospedería directly)

Hostal Anosa Casa
- Rúa Entremurallas, 9
- 42.87701, -8.54457
- ☎ +34 981 585 926
- ✉ reservas@anosacasa.com
- 🏠 www.anosacasa.com
- ♂=40€ ♂♂=61€

Casas Reais P.R.
- Rúa Casas Reais, 29
- 42.88189, -8.54045
- ☎ +34 9 8155 5709
- ✉ reservas@casasreais.es
- 🏠 casasreais.es
- ♂=79€ ♂♂=116€

Mapoula P.R.
- Entremurallas, 10-3º
- 42.87703, -8.54429
- ☎ +34 9 8158 0124
- ☎ +34 6 5957 8122
- ✉ mapoula@mapoula.com
- 🏠 www.mapoula.com
- ♂=39€ ♂♂=121€

Hostal Campo de Estrelas
- Rúa do Pombal nº41
- +34 8 8125 2477
- hostal@campodeestrelas.com
- campodeestrelas.com
- 42.87845, -8.54817
- +34 6 6944 4887
- ♂=50€ ♂♂=70€

Pensión Libredón
- Plaza de Fonseca, 5
- +34 9 8157 6520
- info@libredon.com
- www.acurtidoria.com/pension-libredon
- 42.87960, -8.54499
- ♂=60€ ♂♂=79€

Linares Rooms
- Algalia de Abaixo 34
- +34 9 8194 3253
- linares@grupogescaho.com
- www.linaresroomssantiago.com
- 42.88286, -8.54164
- ♂=66€ ♂♂=75€

Hostal Suso
- Rúa do Vilar, 65
- +34 9 8158 6611
- reservas@hostalsuso.com
- www.hostalsuso.com
- 42.87790, -8.54500
- ♂=60€ ♂♂=60€

Hospedería Tarela
- Praza. da Pescadería Vella, 1
- +34 9 8156 1828
- info@atabernadotarela.es
- www.atabernadotarela.es
- 42.87790, -8.54500
- ♂=59€ ♂♂=59€

Casa Felisa
- Calle Porta da Pena, 5
- +34 981 582 602
- casafelisa@hotmail.com
- www.casafelisa.es
- 42.88272, -8.54345
- ♂=45€ ♂♂=60€

What to see and do when in Santiago?

The Pilgrim's Mass

The pilgrim's mass in Santiago is at 12:00 each day and is a fantastic experience. Whilst it might not to be to everyone's taste or inclination, it is part of the pilgrimage experience and it is worth experiencing at least once. The mass normally lasts about 50 minutes.

Mass in English

Mass in English is held at 10:30am Monday to Sunday (except Wednesday) in the chapel in the Pilgrim's office. This is a lovely mass, normally celebrated by a Salesian priest, Fr. Manny, where everyone is invited to share about their Camino and to ask for prayers. It is often supported by volunteers from the English-speaking chaplaincy who provide a warm welcome to English speaking pilgrims from all over the world. Confession in English or just a chat and a cup of coffee with a member of the English-speaking chaplaincy team are available after mass.

Confession and Plenary Indulgences

Please bear with me on this as this is a difficult topic to explain to Catholics let alone other Christians or people of other or no faith. So, if you are not religiously inclined you may want to skip this section or read it out of curiosity alone. Either way I will try and explain this part of the pilgrimage experience as best I can.

Put simply, the Church teaches that sins (wrong doings against other people) keep people away from God. The Church also teaches that if you simply but honestly say sorry to God (via the priest in Confession) your sins will be forgiven. The church teaches that if your sins are forgiven you will go to heaven. However, you will still have to atone for your sins by spending time after your death in a waiting room called Purgatory before you finally get into heaven. The Church also teaches that you can reduce or eliminate this waiting time by means of what is called a papal indulgence which is given for undertaking a task to atone for your sins while still on earth. There are two types of papal indulgence a partial indulgence which reduces the waiting time or a plenary (full) which eliminates this waiting time. Initially plenary indulgences were only given to those who died on pilgrimage.

What is all this got to do with the Camino? Well in 1122, Pope Calixtus II (the Pope who supposedly commissioned the Codex Calixtinus) granted a full (plenary) indulgence for anyone who visited the shrine of Saint James in Santiago de Compostela in the years when the saint's day (July 25th) fell on a Sunday, made a confession whilst there, attended Mass, gave a donation to the upkeep of the shrine and performed good works. This indulgence is still available in a slightly modernised form for anyone who simply visits (there is no need to do a Camino) the Cathedral of Santiago and the tomb of Saint James in a Jacobean Holy Year. These Jacobean Holy Years occur when the feast of Saint James falls on a Sunday – for example 2004, 2010, 2021 and 2027. To complete the qualification for a modern plenary indulgence you must within 15 days either before or after your visit to the Cathedral make a true confession, receive Holy Communion (but not necessarily go to Mass), pray at least the Our Father and the Apostles Creed and pray for the intentions of the Pope. Any visits during the special Holy Year of Mercy (2016) also qualified for the plenary indulgence. But if you can't make it to Santiago during a Holy Year, you can still obtain the indulgence by visiting on one of Saint James's feast days (23rd May, 25th July, or 30th December).

Even if you are of no faith, virtually all priests, whilst not officially administering confession will minister to you and listen in confidence to anything that burdens you.

Confession is available throughout the day at the many confessionals around the cathedral. If there are no priests in the confessionals, or you are seeking confession in your own language, please ask in the sacristy.

The Botafumeiro

The Botafumeiro is one of two giant (1.5 metres tall) incense burners (thuribles) used at the end of the pilgrims' mass to incense the Cathedral. Botafumeiro is a Galician word that literally means "ejector of smoke".

The first recorded use of a large thurible dates from 1322. The current pulley system was designed in the 16th century by Aragon artist Juan Batista Celme. The current Botafumeiro dates from 1851 and was built to replace the even more ornate 15th century Botafumeiro stolen by Napoleon's troops in 1809. It weighs 53kg and can take up to 40kg of charcoal and incense. It travels to a height of 21 metres and up to speeds of 80 km/hr. It is swung on a rope and pulley system by seven men. There are no known fatalities from the Botafumeiro becoming detached from the ropes but there have been several non-fatal accidents in the past where the Botafumeiro did become fully or partially detached. The last of these accidents was in 1937.

The other large thurible, called the La Alcachofa (The Artichoke), is a replica of the one stolen by Napoleon and dates from 1971.

The Botafumeiro is swung on most major holy days. It is not swung every day at the midday mass but since it is such a spectacular sight and one of the highlights of any visit to Santiago, increasingly many groups of pilgrims collect the €450 donation required to secure the swinging of the Botafumeiro or the Alcachofa at the end of the midday mass. If you are part of a group and wish to organise the swinging, the Cathedral ask for one week's notice. The contact for organising the swinging of the Botafumeiro is: botafumeiro@catedraldesantiago.es.

The Pilgrims' Office

The pilgrims' office is where you get your final stamp and your Compostela certificate of completion which is free. Most pilgrims also pay €3 for a certificate of distance and €2 for a round box to take your certificate home rolled up safely.

The pilgrims' office moved at the end of 2015 to larger offices to accommodate the ever-increasing number of pilgrims.

To enter the pilgrims' office, you will need to show your pilgrim's passport. As of 2019 a new system has been introduced to the pilgrim's office. Under the new system, you collect a ticket with a queue number and a QR code. You can scan the QR code which will link you to a website which will show the latest queue number being processed. The advantage of this system is that you can wait in a local café rather than being stood for more than two hours in the queue (line). The disadvantage is that the pilgrim office will often refuse to issue tickets from early afternoon on very busy days which means that those with early morning return flights the following morning have missed out on receiving their Compostela. I still prefer to collect my Compostela early in the morning following arrival in Santiago. If you are among the first 10 pilgrims to collect your Compostela that day you will be given a certificate for a free lunch at the Parador! However, this encourages some pilgrims to start queuing outside the pilgrim's office from 6am in the morning in the summer months. Personally, I like to get to the pilgrim office at 08:00 collect my ticket and have a lazy breakfast at the café at the start of the street, periodically checking the website on the phone and return when the queue is within about 10 to 15 of the queue number of my ticket. The website for the queue system is:

catedral.df-server.info

The pilgrims' office is open 08:00 till 21:00 from April till October and from 10:00 till 19:00 for the rest of the year.

As of 2021 a further process has been added to speed up the issuing of Compostela. Under this latest system you are encouraged to scan a QR code on a board outside the pilgrim office which takes you to an online form where you can enter the data used to prepare the statistics prepared by the Pilgrim's office. The data collected includes which Camino you walked, where you started from, your gender, your age, your nationality and your profession. If you do not have a smartphone, you can still complete a paper form with this data. Once you have completed and submitted the data you can collect your queue ticket with the QR code.

The new pilgrims' office includes a post office, a RENFE (the Spanish national railway company) office, an ALSA (the largest of the bus companies) office, a chaplaincy team on the first floor and a branch of the tourist information office.

- Rúa Carretas, 33
- 42.88233, -8.54714
- +34 9 8156 8846
- oficinadelperegrino@catedraldesantiago.es
- oficinadelperegrino.com/en/pilgrims-reception-office

Summer Opening Times: 08:00 till 21:00 April 1st till October 30th
Winter Opening Times: 10:00 till 19:00 November 1st till March 30th

The Cathedral Museum

The entrance to the Cathedral museum is located on the Praza do Obradoiro to the right as you look at the Cathedral. It takes you through the history of the building of the Cathedral which is rich and varied as well as through some of the art and

treasures of the Cathedral. The tour takes at least two hours, and an audio guide is highly recommended.
- Praza do Obradoiro, s/n
- 42.880084, -8.545210
- +34 9 8155 2985
- tickets.catedraldesantiago.es/en-GB/venta-de-entradas

Summer (April till October) Monday to Sunday Opening Times: 09:00 till 20:00

Winter (November till March) Monday to Sunday Opening Times: 10:00 till 20:00

Cost: €6.00 or €4.00 for concessions.

The Pilgrimage Museum

The pilgrimage museum is housed in the beautiful former Banco de Espana building (designed in 1938 but only completed in 1948) located near the south-east corner of the Cathedral buildings. The museum covers 3 floors on the generic theme of pilgrimage but mainly focused on the history of the Camino. On the top floor you get a good view of the top of the Cathedral which is quite impressive. A tour of the museum should take about an hour. This is my personal favourite amongst the museums in Santiago.
- Praza das Praterías, 2
- 42.87995, -8.54415
- +34 9 8156 6110
- difusion.mdperegrinacions@xunta.es
- museoperegrinacions.xunta.gal

Monday to Friday Opening Times: 09:30 till 20:30
Saturday Opening Times: 11:00 till 19:00
Sunday and Public Holidays Opening Times: 10:15 till 14:45
Cost: €2.40 or €1.20 with your Compostela. Also, free Saturday afternoon from 14:30 and all-day Sunday and for over 65s.

The Galician Museum of Modern Art

This modern buildings dates from 1993. Personally, I like the granite facade and its clean lines, but it is not to everyone's taste. The museum's permanent collection mainly focuses on Galician, Spanish, Portuguese and Latin American artists.
- Rúa Valle Inclán, 2
- 42.88251, -8.53945
- +34 9 8154 6619
- cgac.prensa@xunta.gal
- cgac.xunta.gal

Tuesday to Sunday Opening Times: 11:00 till 20:00
Closed Mondays

Cost: Free.

"Free" Walking Tours of Santiago

The walking tours leave at 10:00 and 11:00 from the Praza do Obradoiro (the biggest of the four squares around the Cathedral and the one with the Parador in it). There will probably be several tour guides each holding an umbrella and you just have to check that the tour is in English (which most are). The tours are "free" in the sense there is no obligation to pay the guide anything, but the expectation is that you give the tour guide a generous tip at the end of the tour depending on how much you thought the tour was worth. The tours last about two hours and I think provide a good balance between the background and history of Santiago. The tour starts slowly but there is quite a bit of walking involved. Overall highly recommended if you have the time.

The restaurants

There are good restaurants all over Santiago, but the main restaurant area is Rúa da Raiña and Rúa do Franco which both lead directly south from the Cathedral both parallel to Rúa do Vilar (where the pilgrims' office used to be). There is so much good seafood, meat and cheese in Santiago it is hard to highlight just one or two dishes. But for me my favourite is the gambas al ajillo (prawns fried in garlic infused olive oil) which I have tried across much of Spain but always seems to taste best in Santiago.

My favourite restaurant, however, is to be found outside of the main restaurant area, southwest of Praza do Obradoiro and is called Restaurante San Clemente. Beware the tapas are the most generous in Santiago and can easily fill you up before you can order a proper meal.

- Rúa de San Clemente, 6
- 42.87915, -8.54702
- +34 9 8156 5426
- www.restaurantesanclemente.com

The bars

There are great bars all over Santiago. But a couple stand out for me:

Cafe Casino/The Bistro. Dating from 1873, this is a fabulous example of an early Art Noveau café, its beautiful wood panelling points to times of former glory. It has a reputation for some of the

best coffee in Santiago, but it also has a very extensive gin menu (with some great guest gins which don't make it on to the main menu and you may need to ask after). It is expensive and the food and particularly the service are variable, but it is still one of my favourite places to visit in Santiago.
- Rúa do Vilar, 35   - 42.87864, -8.54454
- +34 9 8157 7503

Cafetería Paradiso. This hidden gem is only a few doors down from the Cafe Casino. but it is family run and has better food, better service and better prices than the Cafe Casino. While the decor may not compete with the Cafe Casino for grandeur, this bar definitely oozes old world charm.

It is also worth noting that Cafeteria Paradiso does a particularly fine and exceptionally generous gambas al ajillo.
- Rúa do Vilar, 29   - 42.87879, -8.54445
- +34 9 8158 3394

Santiago de Compostela tourist information centre

The tourist information centre is situated on Rúa Vilar which is the road that leads south from the cathedral. It is about 250 metres south of the fountain on the south side of the cathedral on the left-hand side as you walk down.

The staff are exceptionally helpful and can help you find accommodation, bus and train timetables, how to get to the airport, day trips and details of the many places to see and visit while in Santiago. I used to recommend this as being the third of places to check out when you arrive, with the cathedral being number one and the pilgrims' office number two. However, the introduction of the tourist information centre at the pilgrim office now gives you a one-stop opportunity to sort out your stay in Santiago.
- Rúa do Vilar, 63   - 42.87797, -8.54497
- +34 9 8155 5129
- info@santiagoturismo.com   www.santiagoturismo.com

Monday to Sunday Opening Times: 09:00 till 21:00 (May to October)

Monday to Friday Opening Times: 09:00 till 19:00 (November to April)

Saturday, Sunday, Holy Days Opening Times: 09:00 till 14:00 and 16:00 till 19:00 (November to April)
Monday to Sunday Opening Times: 09:00 till 19:00 (Easter)

Finisterre (Fisterra)

Finisterre translates from Latin meaning the end of the earth and for people of Roman and pre-Roman times, the wild rugged coast at one of the most western points of the known world at the time must have literally felt it was the end of the earth. Even today that feeling of being right at the end of the earth resonates. Many pilgrims feel they have not completed their Camino until they have walked the extra three or four days to Finisterre. However, many pilgrims will not enjoy the luxury of an extra four days to extend their Camino to Finisterre but for these pilgrims and the many visitors to Santiago there are numerous day trips available to Finisterre. These day trips are normally guided coach trips which leave Santiago about 9am and return about 6 or 7pm so they are a long day. These guided tours cost in the range of 35 to 50 euros and usually include a visit to Muxía (with its Sanctuary of the Virgen de la Barca where the final scenes of the film The Way were filmed) and Ézaro (where the waterfall falls directly into the ocean). This is an expensive day trip, but the scenery is spectacular and makes it worthwhile.

The remains of Saint James in the Crypt of the Cathedral

Everybody goes up stairs above the altar to hug the statue of St James but not quite as many make the trip downstairs below the altar to visit the remains of Saint James. I think this is a bit of a shame as the few moments you get before the remains of Saint James can be among the most calming and prayerful of your whole Camino. Having said that, I do not want to diminish those who have no religious feelings as the Camino is a great experience for all and even if you do not want to participate in any of the religious aspects, I still believe the Camino is a fabulous experience on and of its own.

Chapter 10 - Background

Statistics

Pilgrim Numbers starting in Sarria by Month

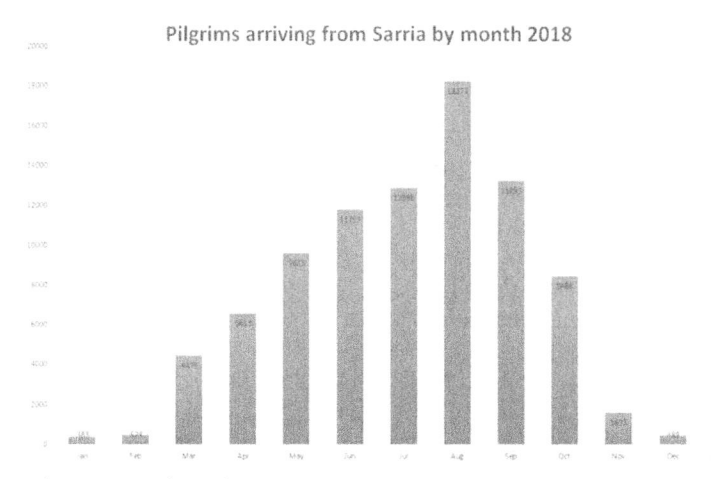

Pilgrims arriving from Sarria by month 2018

Pilgrim Numbers by Year

Pilgrim Numbers by Year

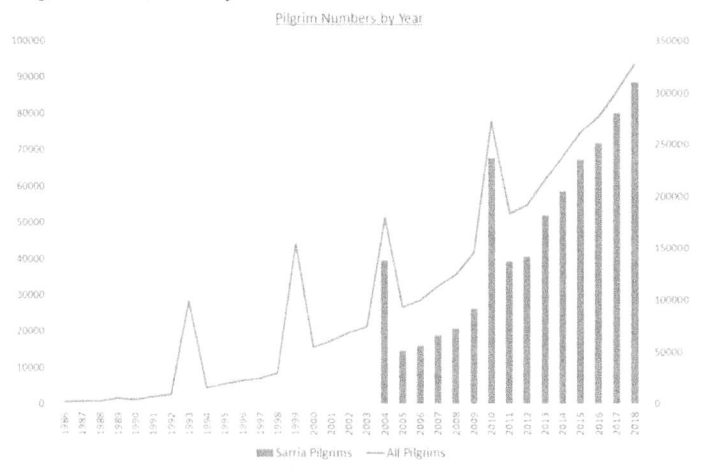

History

A brief history of the Remains of Saint James

There are two apostles called James both saints. The Saint James in Santiago is also known as James the Greater, not because he is deemed to be a better saint than James the Less but because he was simply taller that James the Less. James was one of the fishermen called by Jesus along with his brother John. James and John were sons of Zebedee and Salome. He and John were the first apostles to be called. James was one of the chosen apostles to witness the Transfiguration of Jesus. Tradition holds that after the Resurrection that James went to the Roman province of Hispania (modern day Spain and Portugal) to spread the Gospel. It is held that St James first preached in Galicia in the port of Iria Flavia (modern day Padrón, now more famous for its delicious green peppers). He returned to the Holy Land where he was beheaded by Herod Agrippa in AD 44 and was the first of the apostles to be martyred as recorded in the Acts of the Apostles 12:2. Tradition holds that his body was taken from Jerusalem by his followers, Theodore and Athanasius back to the land where he had spent most of his ministry and which he had grown to love. It is believed that his body was bought back ashore at Iria Flavia. The story goes that Theodore and Athanasius approached the local King for permission to bury St James's body somewhere appropriate. However, the King's wife, Queen Lupa who was not keen on her husband's conversion to Christianity sent Theodore and Athanasius to collect two oxen to pull the wagon with St James's body to a suitable resting place in the countryside (Santiago). The oxen were in fact wild bulls which Queen Lupa had hoped would do away with Theodore and Athanasius and any devotion to the remains of St James. However, the wild bulls were miraculously tamed and upon seeing this, the legend holds that Queen Lupa was also converted to Christianity and dedicated the rest of her life to doing good deeds.

A brief history of the Camino

There are some written references about the remains of St James being buried in Galicia during the Dark Ages. This written evidence of the belief that St James was buried in Galicia dates from at least two hundred years prior to the discovery of the remains in Santiago.

The remains of St James remained undiscovered for over seven centuries until 813 when according to legend a hermit named Pelayo had a vision repeated over several evenings. According to the legend Pelayo lived in a place called Solovio, in the forest of Libredón in what is believed to be the current day site of the church of San Félix de Solovio. This church is to be found in Praza de San Fiz de Solvio which is just a few hundred metres southeast of the Cathedral in modern day Santiago de Compostela. The dazzling vision revealed to Pelayo was of a mysterious blaze above a mound in the forest which gave the impression of a field of stars (Compostela literally translates to field of stars). This vision occurred in what is now the site of the Cathedral of Santiago (Santiago is Galician for Saint James). Hence Santiago received the name Santiago de Compostela (Saint James of the Field of Stars). Pelayo went to the local bishop Teodormiro and told of his vision. Teodormiro prayed and fasted for guidance and then went to Santiago and discovered a sepulchre containing 3 bodies. After various miracles Teodormiro pronounced this to be the remains of Saint James and his two faithful followers Theodore and Athanasius. He relayed his findings to King Alfonso II of Asturias (791-842) who ordered the building of the first church on the site in 834. There are some problems with this version of events not least of which was that Teodormiro did not become bishop till 819. It is thought the 813 date may be an attempt to link the start of the Camino to the Emperor Charlemagne (800-814). In the Charlemagne version of the discovery of the tomb of Saint James, Saint James appeared in a dream to Charlemagne and asked Charlemagne to liberate the lands held and open the way to his tomb.

Gaining in popularity is a tradition that the Camino itself predates the Way of Saint James and that in pre-Christian times that the Camino was a spiritual trail which follows a path of stars within the Milky Way that leads to the end of the earth at Finisterre.

Whatever the exact origins of the discovery of the tomb of Saint James, over the following 400 years visions of Saint James were reported at every important battle during the Christian re-conquest of Spain culminating in a vision during the decisive battle of Las Navas de Tolosa in 1212. As a result of these visions Saint James became the central figure in the re-Christianisation of Spain and eventually became the patron saint of Spain.

The first documented pilgrimage to Santiago was in 950 and this date is viewed as the start of the Camino. The importance of the Camino of Santiago grew massively from the 10th century and by the 13th century it rivalled both Rome and Jerusalem. To try and understand the importance of the Camino in Middle Ages, it is worth noting that at its peak Santiago had half a million pilgrims a year when the population of Europe was only 70 million at a time when most people never left the village, they were born in. In modern day terms this would represent over five million pilgrims per year compared to the 350 000 pilgrims a year who currently make a pilgrimage to Santiago. During the Middle Ages, the trade pilgrimage generated made Santiago one of the wealthiest and finest cities in the world. The reformation started a gradual but profound decline in pilgrims. But it was the hiding of and subsequent loss of the remains of St. James in 1589 from a feared invasion by Sir Francis Drake that put the Camino in abeyance for more than three centuries.

The rebirth of interest in the Camino has been attributed to many factors including the decline of formal worship in Spain but for this author and for many others the introduction to the Way of Saint James had its foundation in the Brazilian author, Paulo Coelho's 1987 spiritual novel "O Diário de Um Mago" ("The Pilgrimage"). As can be seen from the statistics the Camino has gained growing popularity since the early 1990s. This has been further fuelled in the English-speaking world by Emilio Estevez's inspirational 2011 film "The Way". Whatever reason causes you to take that first step on the Way of Saint James, this author prays that you too experience the same wonder and the beauty that he experienced on his first Camino.

Finally, I really hope this guidebook has been of help to you in making your Camino. If there is anything you would like to change or add to this guide to improve it for future pilgrims, please let me know by email at mm3guides@gmail.com.

¡Buen Camino!
Mark McCarthy,
May 30th, 2015.   Updated February 20th, 2023.

Notes and Contacts

Notes and Contacts